Distributed Creativity

"This is an accessible and highly enlightening introduction to the blockchain phenomenon. It reveals why we need to understand blockchain, not just as technology, but as agent of economic and social change, and as a potentially radical transformer of the business of creativity and culture. As an account of the opportunities—and possible costs—of blockchain technology, this lucid and well-researched book offers a terrific primer for those keen to learn more about the emergent 'internet of value' and its effects on music, media and cultural industries production."

—Mark Banks, *Director, CAMEo Research Institute for Cultural and Media Economies, University of Leicester, UK*

"Blockchain is undoubtedly one of the most important emerging technology trends within the creative industries as it allows for new means by which to create, charge for and distribute pieces of work that have traditionally been controlled by large structures. This book covers these topics in a well-thought out manner by an author with both depth and breadth of knowledge. Marcus' insight into these areas is well worth reading and re-reading."

—Cathy Mulligan, *Visiting Researcher, Centre for Cryptocurrency Research and Engineering, Imperial College London, UK*

"Whether you're an A-list musician or an Instagram photo hobbyist, O'Dair's concise yet comprehensive survey of blockchain technology's opportunities and challenges will prepare you for a new economic model that could redefine how we value, exchange and produce creative works."

—Michael Casey, *co-author of* The Truth Machine: The Blockchain and the Future of Everything *and Senior Advisor to the MIT Media Lab's Digital Currency Initiative*

"The great strength of Marcus O'Dair's Distributed Creativity is that it takes the reader beyond the usual 'blockchain as a financial technology phenomenon' into the interesting and important domain of the creative industries. Helpfully, its focus is on analysis and implications and not the technology, elucidating opportunities and benefits, barriers to and risks of adoption as well as providing a set of insightful policy recommendations. Sober, lucid and engaging, this monograph deserves to become an important resource for readers concerned either with the creative industries or blockchain technology itself."

—Richard Adams, *Reader in Entrepreneurship, Bettany Centre for Entrepreneurship, Cranfield University, UK*

"O'Dair's book is a timely and important intervention considering the possibilities of blockchain for the creative industries. Tight and compact, and drawing upon interviews with key stakeholders, it provides a useful critical overview of underpinning technology whilst developing innovative theoretical takes and outlining policy recommendations. Importantly, the legal grey area of this most disruptive of technologies, and its challenges to the 'barbed wire' of copyright law is tackled, and O'Dair makes a convincing argument, echoing Gil Scott Heron, that the revolution will be distributed."

—Guy Osborn, *Professor of Law, University of Westminster, UK*

"This is an exciting and provocative look at a technology-enabled future for the creative industries. Blockchain has disrupted the financial services sector significantly; O'Dair charts in well-thought-through detail the way that the creative industries too might experience a new democratising and disruptive wave of innovation."

—Jeremy Silver, *CEO, Digital Catapult*

"In this important book, Marcus O'Dair leads the way in defining what blockchain and distributed ledger technologies will mean for the creative sector. Beyond the hype, a huge transformation is occurring in the way we operate businesses of all kinds and in how we capture and share value in an online world. Marcus's work is a thoughtful, well-researched and balanced assessment of the notion of 'distributed creativity' and its implications for policymakers as well as for one of Britain's most important economic sectors."

—Helen Disney, *Co-Chair, Committee for Public Good, Policy and Governance, British Blockchain Association*

"With this book Marcus brilliantly describes the opportunities for creative communities and industries to benefit through using blockchain based technology. Cutting through the blockchain hype he draws his conclusions from a series of in depth interviews with creative start-ups employing blockchain to solve issues such as IPR and faster royalty payments. But Marcus also identifies the barriers that need to be overcome, and concludes with wide-ranging recommendations that will allow the full benefits to be realised."

—Phil Godsiff, *Senior Research Fellow, Surrey Centre for the Digital Economy, Surrey Business School, University of Surrey, UK*

Marcus O'Dair

Distributed Creativity

How Blockchain Technology will Transform the Creative Economy

palgrave
macmillan

Marcus O'Dair
Faculty of Arts and Creative Industries
Middlesex University
London, UK

ISBN 978-3-030-00189-6 ISBN 978-3-030-00190-2 (eBook)
https://doi.org/10.1007/978-3-030-00190-2

Library of Congress Control Number: 2018953689

This Palgrave Macmillan imprint is published by the registered company Springer Nature Switzerland AG
The registered company address is: Gewerbestrasse 11, 6330 Cham, Switzerland

For Charlotte, Iris and Coral

Acknowledgements

This book was made possible by a Digital Catapult EPSRC Fellowship (EP/MO29263/1). My thanks to Jeremy Silver, Matt Ward, Rob Learney, Cat Fernandes and all at the Catapult for making my period as researcher-in-residence so enjoyable. I am also indebted, of course, to Maddie Holder, Gabriel Everington, and everyone at Palgrave. My thinking has benefitted considerably from conversations with Richard Osborne, Zuleika Beaven and Robyn Owen (Middlesex University), Phil Godsiff (University of Surrey) Kensuke Ito (University of Tokyo), Simon Taylor (11FS), Barry James (Token Intelligence), Imogen Heap (Mycellia), Cliff Fluet (Lewis Silkin/Eleven), Helen Disney (Unblocked), Austin Earl (Govnet), Nikolas Guggenberger (University of Münster), Rhodri Davies (Giving Thought/Charities Aid Foundation), Jonny Voon (Innovate UK), Cécile Baird (Decentrl) and Zeynep Gurguc (Imperial College London) among others. Members of the Blockchain Research Institute, including Don Tapscott, Hilary Carter and Kirsten Sandberg, have also significantly shaped my understanding of this topic. Finally, my thanks to all interview respondents:

Irina Albita (co-founder, Big Couch and FilmChain)
Phil Barry (founder, Blokur)
Olivier Biggs (Communication and Community Manager, GUTS)
Bryce Bladon (founding team member, CryptoKitties)
Marcelo Garcia Casil (CEO, Maecenas Fine Art)
Daniel Fowler (Strategy and Operations, JAAK)

Andy Grant (Chief Technology Officer, Artos)
Josef Marc (CEO, Publica)
Christine Mohan (co-founder, Civil)
Robert Norton (CEO and founder, Verisart)
Jamie Sly (Community and Content, Big Couch and FilmChain)
Maria Tanjala (co-founder, Big Couch and FilmChain)

Contents

About the Author

Marcus O'Dair is Associate Professor in Music and Innovation at Middlesex University in London, and convenor of the Blockchain for Creative Industries cluster. He is a member of the DLT working group at techUK and the blockchain and DLT committee at BSI. He is an Associate Editor of the Frontiers in Blockchain Journal and his research has appeared in various academic journals and edited books. He has also published a number of industry-facing insight papers, including one for the Blockchain Research Institute, and written for the Guardian, the Independent, the Times, the Financial Times and the Irish Times. He is currently co-editing Mute Records: Artists, Business, History. Different Every Time, his 2014 biography of the musician Robert Wyatt, was a Radio 4 book of the week; it was also shortlisted for the Penderyn music book prize. As one half of Grasscut, Marcus has released three acclaimed albums and performed across Europe. He was formerly a session musician with Passenger.

CHAPTER 1

Introduction

Abstract Although it is sometimes understood as a financial technology phenomenon, blockchain has the potential to transform numerous sectors—including the creative economy. We are entering a new era of *distributed creativity*, with blockchain technology facilitating frictionless licensing and the fair and accurate distribution of revenue from large-scale collaborative projects. Copyright data, currently held in centralised silos, could also be distributed, allowing for a single source of truth—with the result that creators receive just rewards for their work. Automated payments, executed on a blockchain, could dramatically speed up royalty payments, as well as making them more transparent. Finally, a more inclusive approach to data would encourage innovation, allowing entrepreneurs to build new services. There are, however, significant barriers to adoption. Adoption would also bring with it significant risks.

Keywords Blockchain technology · Creative economy · Blockchain opportunities · Blockchain barriers · Blockchain risks

The importance of the creative economy—of industries ranging from music to gaming to architecture—is hard to overstate. The sector is economically significant, contributing £92 billion a year, for instance, to the UK economy (DCMS 2017). To examine the creative economy in economic terms alone, however, is reductive. Firstly, the sector conveys 'soft power' (Nye 2008) like no other. What is Britain if not the home

M. O'Dair, *Distributed Creativity*,
https://doi.org/10.1007/978-3-030-00190-2_1

of Shakespeare and The Beatles and Zaha Hadid and J. K. Rowling and Saatchi & Saatchi and Alexander McQueen? The creative economy is central to what is sometimes known as 'brand Britain' (although Saatchi & Saatchi, surely, could come up a better phrase). I write from a UK perspective, and the UK does tend to punch above its weight in this respect. Yet the centrality of creative works to national image is true of any country in the world. Secondly, the creative economy creates cultural value. Creative works can enhance our health and wellbeing; help overcome discrimination; and enhance our sense of community and of self. This is as true of TV shows and pop songs as it is of so-called 'high art'. And it is priceless.

Digital technology has lowered the barriers to entry for creativity. Many of us now possess the means to record and digitally distribute music, and to make films and podcasts. Yet digital technology has also introduced a number of significant challenges, as I go on to argue. These challenges are most urgent, perhaps, if you make your living in the creative economy but, given the economic and cultural value outlined above, they should also be of serious concern to policy-makers. Finally, these challenges should concern everyone who considers themselves a fan—of art, or theatre, or literature, or TV, or a dozen other creative fields. I say this not only because, presumably, fans want creators to continue to create but also because, in an age of user-generated content (UGC), fans might well be creators themselves—and so might welcome, for instance, easier licensing of music for Youtube videos.

This book examines the potential of blockchain technology—which emerged underpinning the cryptocurrency, bitcoin, but which is now understood to have far broader applications—to solve the problems faced by the creative economy. The book has three core arguments. The first is that blockchain is far more than a financial technology—or fintech—phenomenon. As Morabito (2017, p. vii) shows, blockchain is being deployed in a range of domains and across an ever-increasing range of industries, from insurance and health to the diamond trade—and, indeed, the creative industries. I have suggested elsewhere (O'Dair and Beaven 2017) that blockchain technology could bring about a shift to what, drawing on Benkler (2006), I have called a 'networked record industry' for recorded music. In this book, I develop that argument: since music is by no means the only creative industry that could be transformed by blockchain technology, I suggest we are entering a broader era of *distributed creativity*. In fact, I would argue that much creativity is already much more distributed than we might imagine from the 'lone genius' creator of popular imagination: we can see this from the rise of UGC, and even from the credits on the typical film. Yet blockchain technology can make it easier to license content for derivative works and allow remuneration for large-scale collaboration to be shared between large numbers of individuals. These developments would encourage further creativity. Crucially, blockchain also allows for the distribution of data relating to creative works—which might sound boring, but it is what gets people paid—and for the speeding up (through automation) of payments and licensing. In addition, developers and entrepreneurs could build on top of a more open and inclusive data model, ushering in a second wave of distributed creativity. Fundamental to this notion of distributed creativity are decentralised, rather than centralised, networks. Blockchains, after all, are built on top of the internet—that confluence of social, technological, economic and cultural transformations that gave us the 'networked society' (Castells 2010). The internet, for Castells, was as disruptive as steam and electricity, and many see blockchain technology in a similar light: a classic example of what Schumpeter (2010) calls creative destruction. My first argument, then, is that blockchain technology offers significant opportunities for the creative economy; indeed, it is potentially transformative, both for individual companies and beyond. This is the argument I put forward in Chapter 3.

My second argument is that the adoption of blockchain technology will be subject to a number of macro factors. In Chapter 4, I deploy the PESTLE framework to examine political, economic, social, technological, legal and environmental barriers to adoption. I also utilise the notion of the techno-economic paradigm (Perez 2002)—in particular, the idea that the wealth-creating potential of a given technological revolution is only realised when accompanied by an adequate socio-economic framework. That there is, in some creative industries, already a sense of 'blockchain fatigue' is understandable, given the hype and the existence of some thoroughly unconvincing start-ups (including a few outright scams). Yet it is also dangerous: blockchain *is* a potentially transformative technology, but it is not going to be adopted at scale overnight. As Rogers (2003, p. 1) points out in his classic work on the diffusion of innovations, 'getting a new idea adopted, even when it has obvious advantages, is difficult.' The hype, in fact, could represent the greatest threat to blockchain's long-term prospects (Mulligan et al. 2018).

My third argument is that, like any disruptive technology, widespread blockchain adoption will create losers as well as winners. I examine the risks of adopting blockchain technology in Chapter 5. What might be the unintended consequences of adoption? Which positive externalities, from which third parties currently benefit, might be lost? Could blockchain-based systems, for instance, make it harder for copyright holders to limit infringement? What would be the effect upon blanket licensing of widespread withdrawal from collection societies?

I conclude, in Chapter 6, with seven recommendations for UK policy-makers.

Blockchain Technology

I do not set out, in this book, to provide a detailed discussion of how blockchain technology works, although I provide a brief introduction to the technology in Chapter 2. Instead, the book concerns the application of blockchain technology—specifically, its application in the creative economy. This subject is addressed, albeit in less detail, in the grey literature (see, for instance, Tapscott and Tapscott 2018; Casey and Vigna 2018). It is also addressed in innumerable media articles and white papers, although these tend towards the tech-utopian—and the latter, of course, are inherently promotional. There is, however, relatively little academic literature on the impact of blockchain technology on the creative economy, despite valuable work on blockchains and copyright by De Filippi and Wright (2018), and on blockchains and art by Zeilinger (2016), O'Dwyer (2017), and Lotti (2016). Scholars associated with the Institute of Network Cultures in Amsterdam have made important contributions to the field (Gloerich et al. 2018), as have an overlapping group of researchers and artists centred around the Furtherfield Gallery in London (Catlow et al. 2017). The impact of blockchain technology on the creative economy is also the subject of my own research, as convenor of the Blockchain for Creative Industries teaching and research cluster at Middlesex University in London (O'Dair et al. 2016; O'Dair 2017; O'Dair and Beaven 2017; Ito and O'Dair 2019; O'Dair and Owen, forthcoming; O'Dair, forthcoming). To the best of my knowledge, however, this is the first monograph on the topic.

The Creative Economy

The creative industries have been defined as 'those industries which have their origin in individual creativity, skill, and talent which have a potential for job and wealth creation through the generation and exploitation of intellectual property' (DCMS 1998, p. 3). It was the UK Labour government, specifically DCMS (then the Department of Culture, Media and Sport; today the Department for Digital, Culture, Media and Sport), that first gave policy prominence to the creative industries as a distinct phenomenon. DCMS originally identified 13 constituent sectors, but this figure has subsequently been reduced to nine: advertising and marketing; architecture; crafts; product design, graphic design and fashion design; film, TV, video, radio and photography; IT, software and computer services; publishing; museums, galleries and libraries; and music, performing arts and visual arts (DCMS 2015).

This taxonomy is far from universally accepted—Howkins (2007), for instance, identifies 15 sectors—and the creative industries concept has been widely criticised (Miller 2004; Ross 2007; Cooke and Lazzeretti 2008; O'Connor and Banks 2009). It can be argued both that creative work takes place outside the 'creative industries' and that not all work within the 'creative industries' is truly creative (Hartley et al. 2013). Nesta (2006) propose an alternative model of overlapping subgroupings ('originals', 'content', 'services' and 'experiences'), while Throsby (2001) favours a concentric circles model in which literature, music, the performing arts and the visual arts constitute the sector's creative core. McRobbie (2016) refers instead to the 'culture industries', Hesmondhalgh (2007) to the 'cultural industries'. O'Connor (2016) has argued that we are now in a post-creative industries era and that, for all its good intentions, the creative industries project has ultimately turned culture into a resource for capitalist exploitation. Despite these ambiguities and limitations, however, I use the term 'creative industries' in some places in this book, since the term is used by the UK Government and by industry bodies such as the Creative Industries Federation. I also refer more broadly, following Florida (2014) and Hartley et al. (2015), to the 'creative economy', since it is now acknowledged that 'there is more creative employment outside the creative industries than inside them' (Hartley et al. 2013).

The creative industries share certain characteristics: demand is uncertain; creative workers care about the products they produce; products are vertically differentiated, in that artists differ in skill, originality, proficiency; and creative outputs are time-sensitive but durable—and the rents, typically from numerous small 'lumps', are durable too (Caves 2000). Creative industries are typically risky; experience tensions between art and commerce; have high production costs and low reproduction costs; and create semi-public goods (Hesmondhalgh 2007). As a means of managing these characteristics, creative industries companies typically establish large repertoires of work, so that the rare big hits will compensate for losses made on less successful releases; rely on 'formatting', for instance in the form of sequels; deploy promotion techniques to maximise value; and attempt to introduce 'artificial scarcity' by controlling access to cultural works (Klein et al. 2015, pp. 28–30). The creative workforce is distinctive for its high level of self-employment; the fact that many workers have a 'primary' job in a different industry; and the blurring of boundaries between 'professional' and 'amateur' creators (Flew 2012, p. 5). Artistic labour markets are also known for the prevalence of casualisation, self-employment and the project-based company (Towse 2010). As the DCMS (1998) definition suggests, the creative industries are also centrally concerned with the management of intellectual property (IP): the protection of the application of ideas and information of commercial value (Cornish et al. 2013, p. 6). In particular, copyright, 'a right given against the copying of defined types of cultural, informational and entertainment productions' produced by authors, playwrights, composers, artists and film directors (Cornish et al. 2013, p. 8), underpins both employment and the continued production of cultural work (Klein et al. 2015, p. 30).

In many respects, the creative industries in the UK are thriving. The sector employs over two million people and is growing at twice the speed of the economy as a whole (Garcia et al. 2018, p. 5). Creative occupations are forecast to grow by 5.3% over the next six years—double the projected job growth in the UK economy as a whole (Bakhshi and Yang 2018). For every £1 of GVA generated by the arts and culture industry, an additional £1.30 of GVA is generated in the wider economy; likewise, every job supported by the arts and culture industry supports an additional 1.77 jobs in the wider economy (Cebr 2017). In terms of exports, official figures may underestimate the value of creative digital exports: it has been suggested that the UK's creative industries actually export £46 billion in goods and services—24% higher than the official figure (Young and Cauldwell-French 2018, p. 4).

This is to consider only the UK context. Globally, the creative industries provide close to 30 million jobs and generate almost $2.25 trillion a year: approximately 3% of global GDP (Lhermitte et al. 2015). It is also, of course, to consider only economic value. There is also *cultural* value, which, Throsby (2001, pp. 28–29) argues, we can disaggregate into aesthetic value (the pleasure we take from listening to a song or looking at a painting); spiritual value (the understanding and insight promoted by cultural work); social value (the connections with others, and the sense of identity and place, that the creative economy helps to cultivate); historical value (a sense of the past, embodied in a work of art, helps illuminate the present); symbolic value (the meaning conveyed by cultural objects); and authenticity value (which derives from the originality and uniqueness of a work). In terms of soft power, the ability to achieve outcomes through attraction rather than coercion, the creative economy is also highly significant.

At the same time, as I argue in Chapter 3, the creative economy faces a number of challenges. Many of them, as I also argue in Chapter 3, could potentially be solved using blockchian technology. Of course, the potential may not be realised, as I state in Chapter 4, and blockchains could make things worse rather than better, as I suggest in Chapter 5. Still, use cases are emerging in numerous creative industries. In digital art, McConaghy and Holtzman proposed the use of blockchain technology to provide 'an ownership layer for the internet' back in 2015, and went on to launch Ascribe: an attempt to allow creators to control their own IP which subsequently attracted more than 10,000 users. Also in 2015, the British singer, songwriter, musician and producer Imogen Heap released a song, 'Tiny Human', in collaboration with a blockchain start-up, Ujo; for the first time, payments were distributed automatically to everyone involved in the song. More recently, we have seen the emergence of the Basic Attention Token (BAT) in advertising, which works in conjunction with the Brave browser. Brave records the way in which users spend their time; publishers of attention-grabbing content are then rewarded with BATs. The result? 'Publishers receive more revenue because middlemen and fraud are reduced. Users, who opt in, receive fewer but better targeted ads that are less prone to malware. And advertisers get better data on their spending' (Basic Attention Token 2018). In fashion, meanwhile, the team behind Provenance, a blockchain start-up, have worked with designer Martine Jarlgaard to increase the transparency of the supply chain—thereby 'enabling brands to provide verified information about the materials, processes and people behind products' (Provenance 2018). Uses cases, then, are numerous. I concentrate in this book on music (Blokur, JAAK), ticketing for performing arts (Artos, GUTS), visual arts (Maecenas Fine Art, Verisart), film (FilmChain), publishing (Civil, Publica) and IT, software and computer services (CryptoKitties). Blokur founded Phil Barry, it is notable, previously led Ujo, the start-up that worked with Imogen Heap on 'Tiny Human'.

Methodology

The book is based on a combination of secondary research and interviews I carried out, via email, in May and early June 2018. I quote interview data, where relevant, in the body of the text; in every case, I include the question the respondent was answering and cite the respondent's answer in full. I also include full interview transcripts from every respondent in the appendix, in the hope of demonstrating that I have based my arguments on critical analysis of all available data, rather than a few carefully selected snippets. I also hope that these interviews can serve as mini case studies, illustrating a few possible blockchain applications.

Many of the claims made for blockchain technology in recent years have seemed not only far-fetched but also somewhat abstract—although 2018, we are promised, will be the year of actual use cases. The start-ups profiled in this book are intended as ballast: specific examples of how this nascent and much-hyped technology might actually be deployed in the creative economy, and the advantages, and possible frustrations, that result. My respondents, selected as representative of a number of different creative industries, were approached via email and gave their informed consent in writing; all were informed that their participation was voluntary and that they had the right to withdraw at any time. Respondents were not paid to participate, although may of course derive some promotional value from their participation. All respondents were offered the option of anonymity, although none have taken it.

The primary research is based on structured interviews; asking the same questions in the same order, I hope, makes it easier to compare and contrast the answers. There are disadvantages to the email interview, in that it is harder to build up a rapport with respondents and impossible to read body language. However, there are also significant advantages. My respondents live and work all over the world; email allowed me to interview them all in a consistent fashion. Email interviews are also less burdensome for busy start-ups, since respondents can participate at a time of their own convenience. Overall, I would argue that the fact that respondents have more time to consider their replies is also an advantage. Finally, email interviews are more efficient as they remove the need for transcription. I have made only extremely minor alterations to respondents' replies to ensure consistency in spelling, punctuation and grammar.

Arguably, conducting interviews via email has increased the diversity of responses. In one case, for instance, more than one company representative has answered my questions; elsewhere, answers are in the form of bullet points rather than full sentences. Although I did provide approximate word counts for replies, some answers are also significantly briefer than others. This would be a significant challenge for quantitative research, but I deploy structured interviews as part of a qualitative methodology.

To scaffold my analysis, I deploy the PESTLE framework in chapters four and five. I also utilise two other important frameworks. Firstly, in examining the advantages and disadvantages of adopting blockchain technology for individual companies, I draw on the 'business model canvas' developed by Osterwalder and Pigneur (2010). In my interviews, however, I condense the business model framework into four, rather than nine, components: *value proposition(s)*, concerning the reason(s) a specific group of customers come to a company rather than its competitors; *market*, concerning a businesses' customers and its ways of interacting with those customers before, during and after a sale; *operations*, concerning a business's structure, day-to-day activities and assets; and *finances*, concerning the ways in which a company makes and spends money. Secondly, I argue that, although the technology can be critical to the value propositions and—in some cases—the revenue streams of individual companies, the transformative potential of blockchain technology cannot be fully realised within single organisations. Accordingly, I deploy the notion of the 'value system' (Porter 1985) to refer to the value chain as it extends beyond the individual company. (Some refer to this, broader, process as a 'value chain', but that term, as used by Porter, in fact refers only to processes within an individual firm.) A value system, then, is the larger stream of activities within which a firm's value chain exists, from suppliers right through to buyers.

Certainly, further research in this area is needed before drawing definite conclusions. I only interviewed representatives of ten start-ups, for instance, and did not interview incumbents or other stakeholders; there is also a role here for quantitative research methods. And although I left my interviews as late as possible in order to ensure that data was as up-to-date as possible, the landscape is changing fast.

Conclusion

To summarise, then, blockchain technology is potentially transformative for the creative economy. At the same time, there are significant barriers to adoption. There are also significant risks. I examine the opportunities, barriers and risks in the following chapters, basing my analysis on secondary research and on structured interviews with representatives of ten start-ups in a range of creative industries, all of whom are utilising the technology.

I conclude this introduction with a disclaimer and a declaration. The disclaimer is as follows: nothing in the book should be taken as investment advice. Readers seeking such advice should seek a duly licensed professional. And the declaration? At the time of writing, I do not hold tokens (or any other stake) in the companies I examine in this book. This might not be good for my bank balance but it does, at least, allow me to write about this space with relative impartiality.

References

Bakhshi, H., and L. Yang. 2018. Creativity and the Future of Work. Nesta. http://www.nesta.org.uk/sites/default/files/creativity_and_the_future_of_work_1.1.pdf. Accessed 2 May 2018.

Basic Attention Token. 2018. https://basicattentiontoken.org/index/. Accessed 1 July 2018.

Benkler, Y. 2006. *The Wealth of Networks: How Social Production Transforms Markets and Freedom*. New Haven and London: Yale University Press.

Casey, M., and P. Vigna. 2018. *The Truth Machine: The Blockchain and the Future of Everything*. London: Harper Collins.

Castells, M. 2010. *The Rise of the Network Society: The Information Age: Economy, Society and Culture*, vol. 1, 2nd ed. Oxford: Wiley-Blackwell.

Catlow, R., M. Garrett, N. Jones, and S. Skinner (eds.). 2017. *Artists Re:Thinking the Blockchain*. Liverpool: Liverpool University Press.

Caves, R. 2000. *Creative Industries: Contracts Between Art and Commerce*. Cambridge, MA: Harvard University Press.

Cebr. 2017. Contribution of the Arts and Culture Industry to the UK Economy. Report for Arts Council England.

Cooke, P., and L. Lazzeretti (eds.). 2008. *Creative Cities, Cultural Clusters and Local Economic Development*. Cheltenham: Edward Elgar.

Cornish, W., D. Llewelyn, and T. Aplin. 2013. *Intellectual Property: Patents, Copyright, Trade Marks and Allied Rights*, 8th ed. London: Sweet and Maxwell.

DCMS. 1998. Creative Industries Mapping Document. https://www.gov.uk/government/publications/creative-industries-mapping-documents-1998. Accessed 20 June 2018.

DCMS. 2015. Economic Estimates 2015. https://www.gov.uk/government/statistics/dcms-sectors-economic-estimates-2016. Accessed 20 June 2018.

DCMS. 2017. DCMS Sectors Economic Estimates 2016: Gross Value Added https://assets.publishing.service.gov.uk/government/uploads/system/uploads/attachment_data/file/662958/DCMS_Sectors_Economic_Estimates_2016_GVA.pdf. Accessed 2 May 2018.

De Filippi, P., and A. Wright. 2018. *Blockchain and the Law: The Rule of Code.* Cambridge, MA: Harvard University Press.

Flew, T. 2012. *The Creative Industries: Culture and Policy.* London: Sage.

Florida, R. 2014. *The Rise of the Creative Class Revisited.* New York: Basic Books.

Garcia, M., J.J. Klinger, and K. Stathoulopoulos. 2018. Creative Nation: How the Creative Industries Are Powering the UK's Nations and Regions. Nesta. https://www.nesta.org.uk/sites/default/files/creative_nation-2018.pdf. Accessed 2 May 2018.

Gloerich, I., G. Lovink, and P. De Vries (eds.). 2018. *Moneylab Reader 2: Overcoming the Hype.* Amsterdam: Institute of Network Cultures.

Hartley, J., W. Wen, and H. Li. 2015. *Creative Economy and Culture: Challenges, Changes and Futures for the Creative Industries.* London: Sage.

Hartley, J., J. Potts, S. Cunningham, T. Flew, M. Keane, and J. Banks. 2013. *Key Concepts in Creative Industries.* London: Sage.

Hesmondhalgh, D. 2007. *The Cultural Industries*, 2nd ed. London: Sage.

Howkins, J. 2007. *The Creative Economy*, updated edition. London: Penguin.

Ito, K., and M. O'Dair. 2019. A Critical Examination of the Application of Blockchain Technology for Intellectual Property Management. In *Business Transformation through Blockchain*, ed. H. Treiblmaier and R. Beck. Basingstoke: Palgrave Macmillan.

Klein, B., G. Moss, and L. Edwards. 2015. *Understanding Copyright: Intellectual Property in the Digital Age.* London: Sage.

Lhermitte, M., B. Perrin, and S. Blanc. 2015. Cultural Times: The First Global Map of Cultural and Creative Industries. Ernst & Young Global Limited. http://www.ey.com/Publication/vwLUAssets/ey-cultural-times-2015/$-FILE/ey-cultural-times-2015.pdf. Accessed 2 May 2018.

Lotti, L. 2016. Contemporary Art, Capitalisation and the Blockchain: On the Autonomy and Automation of Art's Value. *Finance and Society* 2 (2): 96–110.

McConaghy, T., and D. Holtzman. 2015. Towards an Ownership Layer for the Internet. https://d1qjsxua1o9x03.cloudfront.net/live/trent%40ascribe.io/ascribe%20whitepaper%2020150624/digitalwork/ascribe%20whitepaper%20 20150624.pdf?Signature=vYXP8xE9V1J%2Bsc%2FLFVLiQxf3dgg%3D&-Expires=1532152166&AWSAccessKeyId=AKIAIVCZJ33WSCBQ3QDA&-response-content-disposition=inline%3B%20filename%3DTowards%2Ban%2BOwnership%2BLayer%2Bfor%2Bthe%2BInternet%252C%2BV1.03%252C%2B20150624-Trent%2BMcConaghy%2Band%2BDavid%2BHoltzman.pdf. Accessed 1 July 2018.

McRobbie, A. 2016. *Be Creative*. Cambridge: Polity.

Miller, T. 2004. A View from a Fossil: The New Economy, Creativity and Consumption—Two or Three Things I Don't Believe In. *International Journal of Cultural Studies* 7 (1): 55–66.

Morabito, V. 2017. *Business Innovation Through Blockchain: The B3 Perspective*. Cham: Springer.

Mulligan, C., J.Z. Scott, S. Warren, and J.P. Rangaswami. 2018. *Blockchain Beyond the Hype*. World Economic Forum. http://www3.weforum.org/docs/48423_Whether_Blockchain_WP.pdf. Accessed 2 May 2018.

Nesta. 2006. Creating Growth: *How the UK Can Develop World Class Creative Business*. London: Nesta. https://www.nesta.org.uk/report/creating-growth/. Accessed 20 June 2018.

Nye, J. 2008. Public Diplomacy and Soft Power. *The Annals of the American Academy of Political and Social Science* 616 (1). JSTOR. http://www.jstor.org/stable/25097996.

O'Connor, J. 2016. After the Creative Industries: Why We Need a Cultural Economy. *Platform Papers* 47: 1–60.

O'Connor, J., and M. Banks. 2009. Introduction: After the Creative Industries. *International Journal of Cultural Policy* 15 (4): 365–373.

O'Dair, M. 2017. How Blockchain Is Transforming the Creative Industries: Copyright and Rights Management in the Second Era of the Internet. Blockchain Research Institute.

O'Dair, M. Forthcoming. Tokens and Techno-Economic Paradigms: On the Value of Blockchain Technology to the Music Industries. In *Music by Numbers: The Use and Abuse of Statistics in the Music Industry*, ed. D. Laing and R. Osborne. Bristol: Intellect.

O'Dair, M., and Z. Beaven. 2017. The Networked Record Industry: How Blockchain Technology Could Transform the Record Industry. *Strategic Change* 26 (5): 471–480.

O'Dair, M., and R. Owen. Forthcoming. Financing New Creative Enterprise Through Blockchain Technology: Opportunities and Policy Implications. *Strategic Change*.

O'Dair, M., Z. Beaven, D. Neilson, R. Osborne, and P. Pacifico. 2016. Music on the Blockchain. https://www.mdx.ac.uk/__data/assets/pdf_file/0026/230696/Music-On-The-Blockchain.pdf. Accessed 24 March 2018.

O'Dwyer, R. 2017. Does Digital Culture Want to Be Free? How Blockchains Are Transforming the Economy of Cultural Goods. In *Artists Re:Thinking the Blockchain*, ed. R. Catlow, M. Garrett, N. Jones, and S. Skinner. Liverpool: Liverpool University Press.

Osterwalder, A., and Y. Pigneur. 2010. *Business Model Generation*. Hoboken: Wiley.

Perez, C. 2002. *Technological Revolutions and Financial Capital: The Dynamics of Bubbles and Golden Ages*. Cheltenham: Edward Elgar.

Porter, M. 1985. *Competitive Advantage: Creating and Sustaining Superior Performance*. New York: Free Press.

Provenance. 2018. Increasing Transparency in Fashion with Blockchain. https://www.provenance.org/case-studies/martine-jarlgaard. Accessed 1 July 2018.

Rogers, E. 2003. *Diffusion of Innovations*, 5th ed. New York: Free Press.

Ross, A. 2007. Nice Work If You Can Get It: The Mercurial Career of Creative Industries Policy. In *MyCreativity Reader: A Critique of Creative Industries*, ed. G. Lovink and N. Rossiter, 31–49. Amsterdam: Institute of Network Cultures.

Schumpeter, J. 2010. *Capitalism, Socialism and Democracy*. London and New York: Routledge.

Tapscott D., and A. Tapscott. 2018. *Blockchain Revolution: How the Technology Behind Bitcoin and Other Cryptocurrencies Is Changing the World*, updated edition. New York: Penguin Random House.

Throsby, D. 2001. *Economics and Culture*. Cambridge: Cambridge University Press.

Towse, R. 2010. *A Textbook of Cultural Economics*. Cambridge: Cambridge University Press.

Young, S., and E. Cauldwell-French. 2018. The True Value of Creative Industries Digital Exports. Creative Industries Federation. https://www.creativeindustriesfederation.com/sites/default/files/2018-03/Federation%20Cebr%20CIC%20The%20true%20value%20of%20creative%20industries%20digital%20exports.pdf. Accessed 2 May 2018.

Zeilinger, M. 2016. Digital Art as 'Monetised Graphics': Enforcing Intellectual Property on the Blockchain. *Philosophy & Technology* 31 (1): 15–41.

CHAPTER 2

Blockchain: The Internet of Value

Abstract We can think of blockchain technology as representing the 'internet of value (internet 2.0), as opposed to the 'internet of information' (internet 1.0). Alternatively, some see blockchains as part of web 3.0, a decentralised, read-write-execute web that is fundamentally different from web 1.0 (the read-only web, used to search for information) and web 2.0 (the read-write web of user-generated content). Blockchains have also been portrayed as part of the fourth industrial revolution, following the revolutions inspired, respectively, by steam, electricity and information technology. Blockchain technology may indeed represent a technological revolution—but new techno-economic paradigms do not establish themselves overnight. And the price fluctuations of bitcoin, or the various cryptographic tokens, do not directly reflect the value of the underlying technology; in some respects, indeed, they distract from it. It is also a mistake to assume that blockchain is a necessarily radical—and radically disintermediating—technology. Broadly speaking, we can distinguish between incorporative/sustaining and radical/disruptive applications.

Keywords Bitcoin · Blockchain · Smart contracts · DApps · Tokens Tokenomics

M. O'Dair, *Distributed Creativity*,
https://doi.org/10.1007/978-3-030-00190-2_2

From Bitcoin to Blockchain

Blockchain technology emerged as the architecture underpinning a cryptocurrency—a digital currency whose security is guaranteed through the use of cryptography. That cryptocurrency was bitcoin, 'a peer-to-peer electronic cash system' proposed in a 2008 paper by the almost certainly pseudonymous Satoshi Nakamoto and implemented the following year. Bitcoin was radical in its removal of third parties—in that case, banks—through a clever combination of technology and incentivisation. Most ingenious was Nakamoto's solution to the 'Byzantine Generals Problem', which concerns the difficulty of exchanging information over an unreliable and potentially compromised network (Lamport et al. 1982). Bitcoin allows for consensus without requiring an intermediary to verify transactions. Instead, so-called 'miners' validate transactions; since a considerable amount of computational work is required, the system is known as 'proof of work'. Also critical is the 'public key infrastructure', whereby users control two separate 'keys', or strings of numbers and letters: a private key, that we can more or less compare to a PIN code, and a public key that can be shared (Casey and Vigna 2018, pp. 64–65). The result is 'a digital, decentralised, partially anonymous currency, not backed by any government or other legal entity, and not redeemable for gold or other commodity' (Grindberg 2011, p. 160); 'the world's first completely decentralised digital currency' (Brito and Castillo 2016, p. 1).

Bitcoin emerged from the 'cypherpunk' movement of the 1990s, which combined a libertarian outlook with a commitment to powerful cryptography (Narayanan et al. 2016, p. 175). Bitcoin then gained notoriety for its associations with the 'dark net': it was used, for instance, to buy drugs on sites such as Silk Road (Lanchester 2016). More recently, as it has begun to enjoy a reputation as a novel type of speculative asset, bitcoin has been bought by a number of risk-tolerant investors. While so-called 'bitcoin maximalists' continue insist that bitcoin is of interest only as currency, it is now generally agreed that the most important aspect of bitcoin is not the currency itself but its underlying architecture. If bitcoin was the first innovation in this space, agues Gupta (2017), then the second innovation was 'the realisation that the underlying technology that operated bitcoin could be separated from the currency and used for all kinds of other interorganisational cooperation'. Less important than bitcoin, in other words, is the underlying blockchain: 'a revolutionary method to ensure trust among anonymous counterparts in decentralised systems without the need of central, supervisory, authorities in charge of verifying the correctness of the records in the ledger' (Tasca et al. 2017, p. 2).

There is still some confusion over terminology. Some, for instance, use 'blockchain' and 'distributed ledger technology' (DLT) interchangeably (Deshpande et al. 2017), and there are places in which that is true of this book too. Others argue that a blockchain is a particular type of DLT:

> The principle way in which a blockchain is different from other distributed databases is that a blockchain is designed to achieve consistent and reliable agreement over a record of events (e.g., 'who owns what') between independent participants who may have different motivations and objectives. Put in a slightly different way, participants in a blockchain network reach consensus about changes to the state of the shared database (i.e., transactions amongst participants) without needing to trust the integrity of any of the network participants or administrators. (Hileman and Rauchs 2017, p. 13)

Essentially, a blockchain is a type of distributed ledger 'composed of a chain of cryptographically linked "blocks" contained in batched transactions' (Hileman and Rauchs 2017, p. 11); put another way, it is a data structure in which each block not only tells us the value of the previous block but also contains a digest of that value, which allows us to verify that the value hasn't been changed (Narayanan et al. 2016, p. 11). The critical point is that blockchains allow consensus without a trusted intermediary. At the same time, the extent of disintermediation should not be overstated: we can anticipate a thinning of intermediaries, rather than their compete removal.

I do not, here, go into detail about how blockchains work. This in part because there are useful explanations elsewhere (Buterin 2014; Antonopoulos 2015; Swan 2015; Narayanan et al. 2016; Brito and Castillo 2016) and in part because, unless you are a developer, detailed technical knowledge is simply unnecessary. Many of us use the internet every day without understanding TCP/IP. The focus of this book is the *application* of blockchain technology; specifically, its application within the creative economy. This impact, I suggest, could be transformative, even revolutionary. This might seem a bold claim to make of what is, in essence, a new kind of ledger—but only if we forget that the development itself capitalism was underpinned by double-entry bookkeeping. Even money, as Lanchester (2016) points out, is ultimately only entries on a ledger. The notion that you can trust the blockchain while knowing nothing about its users, then, is extremely powerful:

> For the first time in human history, we have a register that does not need to be underwritten by some form of authority or state power, other than itself … A decentralised, anonymous, self-verifying and completely reliable register of this sort is the biggest potential change to the money system since the Medici. It's banking without banks, and money without money. (Lanchester 2016)

If anything, by focusing only on money, Lanchester does not go far enough. Schwab (2016) regards blockchain technology—alongside artificial intelligence, robotics, the internet of things, 3D printing, nanotechnology and biotechnology—as part of the 'fourth industrial revolution'. Gupta (2017), Swan (2015), Mougayar (2016a), and Godsiff (2016) also portray blockchains in revolutionary terms. How can we justify such claims? Not everyone is keen on the analogy, but it has been suggested that we can think of blockchains as doing to ledgers what Google Docs has done to documents: giving multiple parties access to a single version of truth (Mougayar 2016b). The difference, of course, is that blockchains also reduce the need for intermediaries: this is Google Docs without Google. Alternatively, some conceptualise blockchain technology as 'the spreadsheet in the sky', to which anyone can add (at least in the case of bitcoin) and from which nothing can be deleted. Finally, and perhaps most usefully, we can think of blockchain technology as representing the 'internet of value', or the internet 2.0, distinct from the 'internet of information' (internet 1.0) with which we are already familiar (Tapscott and Tapscott 2017).

As an alternate framing device, Lundy et al. (2018) see blockchains as fundamental to web 3.0: 'a re-architecting of the net to assert the core objective of decentralisation that inspired many of the early pioneers who built the internet 1.0' (Casey and Vigna 2018, p. 9). If web 2.0 has been dominated by the likes of Facebook, Uber and Airbnb, web 3.0 is an attempt 'to do away with these intermediaries altogether, letting people forge their own bonds of trust to build social networks and business arrangements on their own terms' (Casey and Vigna 2018, p. 9). Whether we call it the internet 2.0 or web 3.0, this shift is expected to 'upend business models and disrupt industries… [and] challenge how we have structured society, defined value and rewarded participation'

(Tapscott and Tapscott 2017, p. 5). The claims, then, are bold. To fully understand why they might be justified, we have to move beyond bitcoin to what some call 'blockchain 2.0'.

Blockchain 2.0: Smart Contracts and DApps

In the years since Nakamoto's (2008) white paper, we have seen attempts to extend the functionality of the bitcoin blockchain. Counterparty, for instance, allows users to create and trade any kind of digital token. There have also been new blockchains entirely, such as ethereum: a kind of 'global, decentralised *virtual machine*... the first truly extensible platform for building decentralised applications' (Casey and Vigna 2018, p. 80, emphasis in original). There are, in fact, now many hundreds of cryptocurrencies, with bitcoin, bitcoin cash, ether and litecoin among the most prominent. (Why both bitcoin and bitcoin cash? Because, following a dispute over block size, bitcoin split in two in 2017. Ethereum split the same year, into ethereum and ethereum classic.) Although people tend to talk of 'the blockchain', then, there are in fact a number of blockchains in existence.

Broadly, we can distinguish between *permissionless, public, shared systems* that 'allow anyone to join the network, to write to the network and to read the transactions from those networks', and the *permissioned, private, shared systems*, often run by consortia, that have 'whitelisted access, meaning that only those people with permission can read or write to such systems (Mulligan et al. 2018, p. 5). Bitcoin would be an example of a permissionless system; Hyperledger and Corda would be examples of permissioned systems. There are also hybrid systems, that are both *permissioned* and *public*, providing for situations 'where whitelisted access is required but all the transactions should be publicly viewable' (Mulligan et al. 2018, p. 5). Permissioned, private, shared systems have the highest transaction speeds but are also the most centralised; permissionless, public, shared systems, at the other extreme, are the most decentralised but also have the slowest transaction speeds. There are other differences between blockchains too. Some developers, for instance, are exploring alternatives to proof of work, such as proof of stake, which does away with miners and instead takes a 'skin in the game' approach, linking validation to cryptocurrency ownership; the more coins you own, the likelier it is that you will be considered a trusted validator (Tasca et al. 2017, p. 18). One prominent cryptocurrency, IOTA, runs not on a blockchain at all but, rather, on a structure known as a 'tangle' or directed acyclic graph (DAG)—an example of DLT that does not use blocks.

Blockchains have evolved, as well as proliferated. Elsden et al. (2018) present seven classes of blockchain applications: as well as *currency* (such as bitcoin), there is *underlying architecture* (such as ethereum), *financial services*, *proof-as-a-service*, *identify management*, *governance* and, finally, *property and ownership*. Particularly significant is the emergence of so-called 'smart contracts': 'little computer programs [built] directly into blockchain that allowed financial instruments, like loans or bonds, to be represented, rather than only the cash-like tokens of the bitcoin' (Gupta 2017, p. 2). The joke about smart contracts is that they are not smart (or, at least, that they are only as smart as what is programmed into them) and neither, in any legal sense, are they contracts. This is reflected, for instance, in the interview I conducted for this book with Robert Norton, CEO and Founder, Verisart:

> *O'Dair*: What is the biggest misconception about adopting blockchain technology within the creative industries?
>
> *Norton*: Smart contracts and neither necessarily smart nor contracts in a legal sense. They are better described as self-executing code based on pre-agreed parameters.

At the same time, smart contracts are undoubtedly an important development: they are, for Gupta (2017), the third key innovation in this space, following, first, the invention of bitcoin and, second, the recognition of blockchain technology as distinct from that currency. We can think of smart contracts as self-executing software programmes or programmable transactions: cryptographic boxes that automatically unlock when certain conditions are met (Gupta 2017). Although we can trace smart contracts back to Szabo (1997) and Grigg (2004), blockchain technology has given them a new lease of life. Indeed, with smart contracts, we may be moving towards an 'internet of agreements', and a new era of global trade:

> Of course trucks will still break down, and apartments will still have plumbing problems. But the incidental complexity involved in business operations could go down by a very large factor, into a domain where a much more complex, contingent and interwoven business environment will emerge. Such an environment might be as different from today's

> business environment as container shipping is superior to packing boats by hand. It will be better for government, business and people. (Gupta and ConsenSys 2017)

Also crucial to the development of blockchain technology is the concept of DApps, or Decentralised Applications. When we talk about blockchain technology, we are really talking about three layers: the *protocol* layer, the infrastructure upon which the networks and applications are built; the *network* layer, the actual peer-to-peer network that brings a distributed ledger to life by connecting participants; and the *application* layer, the primary user interface (Hileman and Rauchs 2017, p. 26). DApps, sitting at the top of the blockchain tech stack, are the user experience layer. We can think of them as akin to standard apps, except that they run their backend code on peer-to-peer networks. DApps are also typically open source; store data cryptographically; and use tokens (see 'tokenomics' section below) as an incentive method.

To date, the most ambitious use of smart contracts is the Decentralised Autonomous Organisation, conceived as a corporation running without any human involvement under the control of a set of business rules (Swan 2015, p. 24). This is not an abstract thought experiment: an attempt was made to launch such a venture, actually called the DAO, in 2016. As McAfee and Brynjolfsson explain:

> There was no human or institutional layer outside of the DAO's software – no CEO, board of directors, and not even a steering committee like the one Linus Torvalds ran for Linux. The DAO was software and software alone… There was no-one with the formal authority to change the DAO, no-one to negotiate with or appeal to in order to alter it, and no-one to sue or pursue in court if a perceived injustice was perpetrated through it. (McAfee and Brynjolfsson 2017, pp. 302–303)

The DAO was a high-profile project, at the time the most visible in the ethereum ecosystem, and it raised the equivalent of $162 million in 28 days (to cite crypto prices in dollars is fairly standard practice, and I follow it in this book). However, due to serious flaws in its software and economic model, the DAO essentially acted 'like an ATM full of cash that kept dispensing money even though the requesting account had a zero balance' (McAfee and Brynjolfsson 2017, p. 304). An unidentified user removed approximately one-third of the money shortly after the DAO went live. Strictly speaking, this was not a hack but a legitimate exploitation of a feature of the code. The response of the ethereum community was a 'hard fork', which essentially turned back the clock to 'forget' historic transactions. Some, however, refused to abandon their belief in blockchain immutability and 'code as law'. Those who would not accept the hard fork continue to use what is now called ethereum classic. This is why we have two versions of ethereum today.

Tokenomics: Blockchains and Value

The DAO disaster might have permanently damaged ethereum. Instead, it bounced back: at the time of writing, in June 2018, ethereum is trading at over $500 (although this, like every other figure cited in this book, will of course be out of date the moment it is typed). Ethereum classic, by contrast, is trading at around $15. Bitcoin itself is at just over $6600, which is seen as low, given that, at its December 2017 peak, it was around $20,000. In fact, to despair at the current value of bitcoin is to take a short-term view (and to suffer from so-called 'recency bias'). At the start of 2017, one bitcoin was worth less than $1000; back in 2010, 10,000 bitcoins (today worth over $60 million) seemed a reasonable price for two pizzas. The total cryptocurrency market cap, at the time of writing, is close to $300 billion.

The fluctuating price of bitcoin, in particular, has earned it widespread attention as a speculative asset. In fact, although bitcoin is referred to as a cryptocurrency, Birch (2017, pp. 171–172) points out that it is not a reliable store of value; it has limited use as a medium of exchange; and it does not seem to be used as an independent unit of account. For Birch, bitcoin is better understood as a kind of digital commodity. McAfee and Brynjolfsson (2017, p. 288) agree that bitcoin's wild fluctuations make it unsuitable as a means of exchange or as a store of value; it is primarily of interest, they argue, for risk-tolerant investors.

Today, risk-tolerant investors are also purchasing 'tokens', a concept closely associated with the ethereum blockchain. Unlike bitcoin, these tokens are not for general use; instead, they are deployed only within an associated DApp (Casey and Vigna 2018, p. 101). Tokens are most closely associated with token sales, also known as initial coin offerings (ICOs). Essentially, we can understand token sales as crowdfunding campaigns in which an investor receives tokens in return for a cryptocurrency contribution: a kind of crypto pre-sale.

> In an initial coin offering (also known as a token sale), a project team sells its token to the general public for the first time. In some sense, an initial coin offering is simply a Kickstarter-style crowdfunding campaign, which allows the general public to participate in an early-stage project. However, blockchain tokens are usually tradable, while Kickstarter purchases usually are not. By selling tokens to the public across the globe, a project team can raise financial capital to support the development of its project. (Chen 2017)

Tokens, then, are a novel means of raising finance for new ventures. Yet they are not only that. Some make a distinction between *security* tokens, which are tradeable assets, and *utility* tokens, which provide users with access to a product or service. At least for those with utility, tokens reduce the cost not only of bootstrapping a new platform but also, subsequently, of operating it:

> In the first phase – often referred to as a token sale or Initial Coin Offering (ICO) – a native token is used to crowdfund the development of a platform. In the second phase, an incentive system is used to determine the conditions under which contributors can earn tokens for providing the resources needed for the platform's operations... (Catalini and Gans 2017, p. 12)

Most start-ups that regard tokens only as a means of raising capital do not, at present, appear sustainable in the longer term. This is in part because start-ups funded through tokens sales are obliged to act, at seed stage, like a public company, investing heavily in marketing and communication rather than their core product or service. To deploy the business model canvas developed by Osterwalder and Pigneur (2010), then, it is not sufficient to see tokens as only a revenue stream. In fact, a properly designed token will affect other aspects of a company's business model, for instance its customer relationships. This makes sense only for tokens that are likely to be reasonably enduring—tokens, in other words, that have utility. Many token sales to date have been dubious, some outright scams. Some may also be open to legal challenge. Tokens that have utility, however, could be game-changing, and token engineering is now a fast-growing and important field. Token sales provide 'unprecedented liquidity and efficiency for capital formation while minimising transaction cost'; they 'allow promoters to avoid sacrificing equity for financing' and 'provide low barriers to entry for a diverse body of investors and thus increase the diversity and the heterogeneity of start-up funding' (Kaal 2018, p. 2).

At least in the short-term, the overall value of bockchain technology is unrelated to the question of whether we find ourselves in a 'bull' market of rising cryptocurrency prices or a 'bear' market of falling prices. The economic value of blockchain technology is unrelated to minor fluctuations of this or that token, whatever commentators—who may well be holders of those (or rival) tokens—might claim. In fact, Mulligan et al. (2018, p. 3) suggest, the inflated claims often made for particular tokens, and for blockchain technology in general, actually represent a barrier to adoption:

> It has started to seem that the most intractable of the world's problems have merely been waiting for blockchain to arrive. This is not only misleading and untrue but also becomes a barrier to decision-makers in taking a balanced perspective on the technology. The very enthusiasm to (over) promote the technology, therefore, is also the very thing that is damaging its long-term prospects. (Mulligan et al. 2018, p. 3)

This is a useful corrective to the hype. Mulligan et al. (2018) have developed a 'decision tree' to help businesses decide whether or not to adopt blockchain technology—or at least whether or not to adopt it *now*. (Anyone not attempting to remove intermediaries or brokers, for instance, will find themselves firmly instructed not to adopt in step one.) Wüst and Gervais (2017) also present a decision tree intended to help users decide whether or not blockchain technology is appropriate for a given scenario. 'In general,' they conclude, 'using an open or permissioned blockchain only makes sense when multiple mutually mistrusting entities want to interact and change the state of a system, and are not willing to agree on an online trusted third party' (p. 2).

Panic accompanies the hype: some newcomers to bitcoin, for instance, have already jumped ship, scared off by the cryptocurrency's relative price decrease since its December 2017 peak. Such short-term horizons seriously misjudge the significance of the technology. Blockchain, Iansiti and Lakhani (2017) argue, is a foundational technology, with the potential to profoundly change our economic and social system—'but while the impact will be enormous, it will take decades for blockchain to seep into our economic and social infrastructures.' I would argue that Iansiti and Lakhani are too cautious, but several of the respondents I interviewed for this book expect wider adoption to take at least a few years. Blockchain may indeed represent a technological revolution, defined by Perez (2002, p. 8) as 'a powerful and highly visible cluster of new and dynamic technologies, products and industries, capable of bringing about an upheaval in the whole fabric of the economy and of propelling a long-term upsurge of development'. But new techno-economic paradigms do not just appear. As Perez states:

> The irruption of such significant clusters of innovative industries in a short period of time would certainly be enough reason to label them 'technological revolutions'. Yet what warrants the title for the present purposes is that each of those sets of technological breakthroughs spreads far beyond the confines of the industries and sectors where they originally developed. Each provides a set of interrelated generic technologies and organisational principles that allows and fosters a quantum leap in potential productivity for practically all economic activities. (Perez 2002, p. 8)

Viewed through Perez's framework, we are now experiencing the turbulence characteristic of an 'installation period'—a period she divides into 'irruption' and 'frenzy'. Evidence of frenzy is not hard to find, with up to 100,000 new users reportedly signing up to Coinbase, a cryptocurrency exchange, in a single day (Cheng 2017). There are reports of companies adding the word 'blockchain' to their names and immediately doubling (Peters 2017) or even quadrupling (Pham 2017) in value. The current interest in token sales has the hallmarks of a speculative bubble, and commentators have made comparisons to the gold rush and the dot-com bubble (Casey and Vigna 2018, p. 11), even to the tulip mania of the 1630s (Innanen 2017). Yet this is by no means to suggest that crypto investors are fools. Here, too, it is useful to consider a broader historical perspective: Garber (2001, p. ix) argues that historical bubbles such as Dutch tulip mania, the Mississippi Bubble and the South Sea Bubble should not be understood as outbreaks of collective madness. On the contrary, for Garber, 'the most famous aspect of the [tulip] mania, the extremely high prices reported for rare bulbs and their rapid decline, reflects normal pricing behaviour in bulb markets and cannot be interpreted as evidence of market irrationality' (p. 13). 'Bubble', Garber concludes,' is a non-explanation: 'merely a name that we attach to a financial phenomenon that we have not invested sufficiently in understanding' (p. 124).

Incorporative and Radical Applications

There is a misconception that blockchain is a necessarily radical—and radically disintermediating—technology. In fact, Swartz (2017, p. 86) suggests that we can identify two versions of blockchain implementation: *incorporative* (attempts to innovate within the existing system, for instance through increasing efficiency) and *radical* (attempts to bring about a new techno-economic order). In the terms set out by Christensen (2016), we can think of these as *sustaining* (incrementally improving the performance of an established product) and *disruptive* (introducing an entirely new value proposition). Broadly speaking, radical/disruptive applications tend to be aligned with permissionless, public, shared systems, while incorporative/sustaining applications tend to be executed on permissioned, private, shared systems. Swartz suggests that, 'in practice, there is a continuum between the two ideological modes' (p. 87), just as there exist hybrid permissioned/public systems. Yet the incorporative and the radical are in essence fundamentally opposed:

> The incorporative blockchain offers a vision directly opposed to that of the radical blockchain in terms of futurity; decentralisation and disintermediation; and autonomy and automation. Whereas the radical blockchain dream is marked by futurity, the incorporative blockchain dream is slow moving and risk averse. Whereas the radical blockchain dream values decentralisation and disintermediation, the incorporative dream insists on governance and surfaces the work of intermediaries. Whereas the radical dream seeks autonomy built on automation, the incorporative blockchain dream imagines automation as a tool, not a replacement, for human work. (Swartz 2017, pp. 96–7)

The incorporative blockchain dream, for Swartz, 'isn't really a dream at all. It is boring' (p. 96). Yet boring, for many incumbents, is just fine. In fact, according to the theory of value networks, 'the context within which a firm identifies and responds to customers' needs, solves problems, procures input, reacts to competitors, and strives for profit' (Christensen 2016 p. 32), established organisations are inherently inflexible. This is because they are so committed to the needs of their best customers, and to investing most heavily in innovations that promise the highest returns. Christensen argues that, although this serves these companies well when dealing with sustaining technologies, it is catastrophic when disruptive technologies enter the picture. The value networks of established companies simply cannot adapt in time. This resuts in what Christensen calls the *innovator's dilemma.*

The innovator's dilemma gives new entrants an attacker's advantage, resulting not from the technology itself but from the inflexibility of incumbents. In the blockchain space, new entrants are using the technology to do more than reduce costs and transaction latency: rather than solving existing problems, they are starting to create new opportunities (Mouyagar 2016a). It will take time, however, for these start-ups to break through: new entrants, as Porter (1980, pp. 7–13) points out, face significant barriers to entry, in the form of economies of scale, product differentiation, capital requirements, switching costs, access to distribution channels, cost disadvantages independent of scale and, finally, government policy. Incumbent firms can also be expected to resist and retaliate, for instance by leveraging experience and economies of scale (Porter 1980, p. 15).

Conclusion

Although blockchains emerged with bitcoin, we can separate the underlying technology from the cryptocurrency. The fact that blockchains allow consensus without a trusted intermediary is potentially transformative; we can think of blockchain technology as representing the 'internet of value', as opposed to the 'internet of information', and as a critical part of the decentralised web 3.0. Although people talk of 'the blockchain', there are a number of blockchains in existence, and well over a thousand cryptocurrencies. Broadly speaking, these can be divided into *permissionless, public, shared systems* and *permissioned, private, shared systems*, although hybrid systems also exist. Not all use mining and proof-of-work to achieve consensus; some, for instance, are exploring a proof-of-stake approach, which relies on 'skin in the game'. One crucial development is the smart contract, a self-executing software programme. Another is the token, a novel means to raise finance but also to provide access to a product or service. These are exciting developments to be sure, and we may be experiencing the beginning of a technological revolution—but new techno-economic paradigms do not appear in the blink of an eye.

References

Antonopoulos, A. 2015. *Mastering Bitcoin: Unlocking Digital Cryptocurrencies.* Beijing: O'Reilly.

Birch, D. 2017. *Before Babylon, Beyond Bitcoin: From Money That We Understand to Money That Understands Us.* London: London Publishing Partnership.

Brito J., and A. Castillo. 2016. *Bitcoin a Primer for Policy Makers*, 2nd ed. George Mason University: Mercatus Center.

Buterin, V. 2014. A Next-Generation Smart Contract and Decentralised Application Platform. https://whitepaperdatabase.com/ethereum-eth-whitepaper/. Accessed 25 March 2018.

Casey, M., and P. Vigna. 2018. *The Truth Machine: The Blockchain and the Future of Everything.* London: Harper Collins.

Catalini, C., and J. Gans. 2017. Some Simple Economics of the Blockchain. Rotman School of Management Working Paper No. 2984598/MIT Sloan Research Paper No. 5191-16. https://papers.ssrn.com/sol3/papers.cfm?abstract_id=2874598. Accessed 4 May 2018.

Chen, Y. 2017. Blockchain Tokens and the Potential Democratisation of Entrepreneurship and Innovation. Stevens Institute of Technology School of Business Research Paper. https://ssrn.com/abstract=3059150. Accessed 24 March 2018.

Cheng, E. 2017. Bitcoin Gets in on the Post-Thanksgiving Shopping Spree, Surges to New Record Above $9000. *CNBC.* https://www.cnbc.com/2017/11/25/bitcoin-tops-8700-to-record-high-as-coinbase-adds-100000-users.html. Accessed 20 June 2018.

Christensen, C. 2016. *The Innovator's Dilemma: When New Technologies Cause Great Firms to Fail.* Boston: Harvard Business Review Press.

Deshpande, A., K. Stewart, L. Lepetit, and S. Gunashekar. 2017. *Distributed Ledger Technologies/Blockchain: Challenges, Opportunities, and the Prospects for Standards.* London: BSI and Rand Europe.

Elsden, C., A. Manohar, J. Briggs, M. Harding, C. Speed, and J. Vines. 2018. Making Sense of Blockchain Applications: A Typology for HCI. In *Proceedings of the 2018 CHI Conference*, 21–26, April, Montreal. https://chriselsden.files.wordpress.com/2018/01/elsden-making-sense-of-blockchain-applications.pdf. Accessed 4 May 2018.

Garber, P. 2001. *Famous First Bubbles: The Fundamental of Early Manias.* Cambridge, MA: MIT.

Godsiff, P. 2016. Disruptive Potential. In *Distributed Ledger Technology: Beyond Blockchain*, ed. M. Walport. https://www.gov.uk/government/uploads/system/uploads/attachment_data/le/492972/gs-16-1-distributed-ledger-technology.pdf. Accessed 24 October 2017.

Grigg, I. 2004. The Ricardian Contract. http://iang.org/papers/ricardian_contract.html. Accessed 14 May 2018.

Grindberg, R. 2011. Bitcoin: An Innovative Alternative Digital Currency. *Hastings Science & Technology Law Journal* 4: 160–211.

Gupta, V. 2017. A Brief History of Blockchain. *Harvard Business Review*. https://hbr.org/2017/02/a-brief-history-of-blockchain. Accessed 10 November 2017.

Gupta, V., and ConsenSys. 2017. Building the Hyperconnected Future on Blockchains. http://internetofagreements.com/files/WorldGovernmentSummit-Dubai2017.pdf. Accessed 2 May 2018.

Hileman, G., and M. Rauchs. 2017. Global Blockchain Benchmarking Study. https://papers.ssrn.com/sol3/papers.cfm?abstract_id=3040224. Accessed 24 March 2018.

Iansiti, M., and K. Lakhani. 2017. The Truth About Blockchain. *Harvard Business Review*. https://hbr.org/2017/01/the-truth-about-blockchain. Accessed 4 May 2018.

Innanen, A. 2017. Why Today's ICO Craze Resembles the Tulip Mania of the 1630s—And How Things Could Turn Out Better This Time. *Nordic Business Insider*. https://nordic.businessinsider.com/icos-and-tulips-2017-9/. Accessed 20 June 2018.

Kaal, W. 2018. Initial Coin Offerings: The Top 25 Jurisdictions and Their Comparative Regulatory Responses. University of St. Thomas Legal Studies Research Paper No. 18-07. https://papers.ssrn.com/sol3/papers.cfm?abstract_id=3117224. Accessed 4 May 2018.

Lamport, L., R. Shostak, and M. Pease. 1982. The Byzantine Generals Problem. *ACM Transactions on Programming Languages and Systems* 4 (3): 382–401.

Lanchester, J. 2016. When Bitcoin Grows Up. *London Review of Books* 38 (8). https://www.lrb.co.uk/v38/n08/john-lanchester/when-bitcoin-grows-up. Accessed 2 May 2018.

Lundy, L., J. John, H. McLaverty, and S. Noor. 2018. The Convergence Ecosystem: Convergence 2.0—Building the Decentralised Fututre. https://outlierventures.io/wp-content/uploads/2018/03/The_Convergence_Ecosystem_Report_Outlier_Ventures_2018.pdf. Accessed 1 July 2018.

McAfee, A., and E. Brynjolfsson. 2017. *Machine Platform Crowd: Harnessing Our Digital Future*. New York and London: Norton.

Mougayar, W. 2016a. *The Business Blockchain: Promise, Practice and Application of the Next Internet Technology*. Hoboken: Wiley.

Mougayar, W. 2016b. If You Can Understand GoogleDocs, You Can Understand Blockchain. *Coindesk*. https://www.coindesk.com/understand-google-docs-can-understand-blockchain/. Accessed 2 May 2018.

Mulligan, C.J., Z. Scott, S. Warren, and J. P. Rangaswami. 2018. *Blockchain Beyond the Hype*. World Economic Forum. http://www3.weforum.org/docs/48423_Whether_Blockchain_WP.pdf. Accessed 2 May 2018.

Nakamoto, Satoshi. 2008. Bitcoin: A Peer-to-Peer Electronic Cash System. https://bitcoin.org/bitcoin.pdf. Accessed 24 March 2018.

Narayanan, A., J. Bonneau, E. Felten, A. Miller, and S. Goldfeder. 2016. *Bitcoin and Cryptocurrency Technologies: A Comprehensive Introduction*. Princeton and Oxford: Princeton University Press.

Osterwalder, A., and Y. Pigneur. 2010. *Business Model Generation*. Hoboken: Wiley.

Perez, C. 2002. *Technological Revolutions and Financial Capital: The Dynamics of Bubbles and Golden Ages*. Cheltenham: Edward Elgar.

Peters, B. 2017. Long Island Iced Tea Corp. Changes Name to Long Blockchain. *Investor's Business Daily*. https://www.investors.com/news/long-island-iced-tea-corp-has-changed-its-name-to-long-blockchain-stock-soars/. Accessed 4 May 2018.

Pham, L. 2017. This Company Added the Word 'Blockchain' to Its Name and Saw Its Shares Surge 394%. *Bloomberg*. https://www.bloomberg.com/news/articles/2017-10-27/what-s-in-a-name-u-k-stock-surges-394-on-blockchain-rebrand. Accessed 4 May 2018.

Porter, M. 1980. *Competitive Strategy: Techniques for Analysing Industries and Competitors*. London: Free Press.

Schwab, K. 2016. *The Fourth Industrial Revolution*. London: Portfolio Penguin.

Swan, M. 2015. *Blockchain: Blueprint for a New Economy*. Beijing: O'Reilly.

Swartz, L. 2017. Blockchain Dreams: Imagining Techno-Economic Alternatives After Bitcoin. *Another Economy Is Possible: Culture and Economy in a Time of Crisis*, ed. M. Castells. Cambridge: Polity.

Szabo, N. 1997. Formalising and Securing Relationships on Public Networks. *First Monday* 2 (9). http://pear.accc.uic.edu/ojs/index.php/fm/article/view/548/469. Accessed 30 April 2018.

Tapscott, D., and A. Tapscott. 2017. *Realising the Potential of Blockchain: A Multistakeholder Approach to the Stewardship of Blockchain and Cryptocurrencies*. World Economic Forum. http://www3.weforum.org/docs/WEF_Realizing_Potential_Blockchain.pdf. Accessed 10 November 2017.

Tasca, P., T. Thayabaran, and C. Tessone. 2017. Ontology of Blockchain Technologies: Principles of Identification and Classification. https://papers.ssrn.com/sol3/papers.cfm?abstract_id=2977811. Accessed 25 August 2017.

Wüst, K., and A. Gervais. 2017. Do You Need a Blockchain? https://eprint.iacr.org/2017/375.pdf. Accessed 2 May 2018.

CHAPTER 3

Opportunities for the Creative Economy

Abstract Blockchain technology creates a number of significant opportunities for the creative economy. Firstly, as regards *ownership*, blockchains have the potential to improve the process of attribution, allowing creators to receive credit for their work. This ownership information could also be stored in distributed, rather than centralised, databases, helping to provide a single source of truth for payments and licensing. Finally, a large number of parties could feasibly receive royalty payments—even for large-scale projects made up of creators who do not know or trust one another. Secondly, as regards *smart, transparent payments and licensing*, blockchains can automate royalty payments and licensing. These processes can also be made more transparent. Thirdly, blockchains offer *increased control*, allowing creators to set parameters for pricing and licensing their works, and for event promoters to set parameters for the re-sale of tickets. Fourthly, blockchains encourage *new business models*, with consumption data being used to benefit creators rather than intermediaries; cryptocollectibes resulting from digital scarcity; automated *droit de suite* payments; and properly designed tokens.

Keywords Blockchain technology · Intellectual property · Smart contracts · Business models · Digital scarcity · Tokens

M. O'Dair, *Distributed Creativity*,
https://doi.org/10.1007/978-3-030-00190-2_3

Although the creative economy was neglected in the landmark Walport report (2016), Bazalgette (2017, p. 35) states that blockchain technology could 'revolutionise' the creative industries. Certainly, as Bryce Bladon, founding team member at CryptoKitties, points out in our interview, use cases for blockchain technology stretch far beyond financial services:

> *O'Dair*: What is the biggest misconception about adopting blockchain technology within the creative industries?
>
> *Bladon*: The biggest misconception I see is that it is only a technology for engineers, financiers, and Silicon Valley enthusiasts. Blockchain holds immense creative potential, especially in the formal art industry.

To illustrate this potential, I outline twelve specific opportunities below, divided into four broad categories: ownership; smart, transparent payments and licensing; increased control; and new business models.

Ownership

Attribution

'For all of its distribution prowess,' states Howard (2017, p. 21), 'the internet as we know it isn't terribly good at ascribing proper attribution.' The fact that attribution, in the digital world, is so easily lost may be 'the fundamental issue for today's creator' (Howard 2017, p. 144). Intellectual property in general, and copyright in particular, has been 'stretched to breaking point by digital technologies and activities'; 'the digital context has widened and revealed a gulf between copyright law and everyday practices' (Klein et al. 2015, p. 1).

Blockchains can create an unbreakable link between artists and their work, by inextricably linking a data file, for instance a song or a film, to its relevant metadata. Consider Verisart, a start-up that uses blockchain technology to provide 'tamper-proof certificates for art and collectibles' (Verisart 2018). CEO Robert Norton raises blockchain's potential for attribution in our interview:

> *O'Dair*: What do you consider the main benefits that blockchain technology can offer, both to your business and across your industry more broadly?

Norton: Verisart is a simple way for artists to register their works on the blockchain. When an artist creates a work, a digital certificate containing important information such as the artwork image, title, artist name, signature, year of production and materials is encrypted and recorded forever. It helps artists and collectors secure the value of their works and create trusted title. Unlike traditional paper records, these digital certificates of authenticity cannot be duplicated and this significantly reduces the scope for fraudulent activity and fake copies.

At least for most types of creative work, it is not, at present, a case of embedding actual files in a blockchain. Permissionless blockchains, in particular, simply cannot handle that volume of data. Instead, what is added to a blockchain is the 'hash'—a unique identifier made up of a string of letters and numbers—of a work, along with information about the work such as the names of the work's creators and its date of creation. The original data cannot be retrieved from the hash but, as long as file content has not been altered, anyone using the same algorithm will generate the same hash. The files themselves are stored off-chain, for instance on InterPlanetary File System (IPFS). Blockchain-like consensus is necessary only when transferring ownership of assets (Casey and Vigna 2018, p. 238). The blockchain, then, is storing 'references to files available elsewhere, such as on separate peer-to-peer file sharing or overlay networks' (De Filippi and Wright 2018, p. 119). The result is a time-stamped, permanent record of the work and its authorship. 'Just as blockchains can create unique, digital assets out of currency tokens and hashed documents,' suggest Casey and Vigna (2018, p. 228), 'they might also give the same quality to [creative] content' such as digital photos:

> The essential point is that by attaching metadata about the artist, the date of creation, the title of the piece, and other details to the digital work and then immutably registering it to a blockchain transaction, it's possible to turn something that's now completely replicable and untraceable into a uniquely defined piece of property whose journey around the internet can be followed and managed. (Casey and Vigna 2018, p. 232)

Provenance, coupled with digital scarcity, gives rise to the phenomenon of cryptocollectibles (see 'digital scarcity' below). Using blockhain technology to register creative works could also help to unlock the value in orphan works: creative works that are subject to copyright for which one or more of the rights holders is either unknown or cannot be found. Finally, blockchains can be used to record other forms of IP: Cognate, for instance, is using blockchain technology to create a timestamped, permanent record of trademarks.

Distributed IP Databases

Copyright information is currently stored in centralised, siloed databases. These are typically incomplete; at times, they actually conflict. In the music industry, there have been attempts to build a comprehensive database, most notoriously, the Global Repertoire Database (GRD), but these have failed, ultimately, because of a failure to align incentives.

Blockchain technology can provide a distributed, networked alternative to centralised and siloed IP databases: a single source of truth as to who has the rights to a given song or piece of archive film footage. Why might this succeed when previous attempts at creating a global database, such as the GRD, failed? Because blockchains align incentives: they offer a way to encourage 'a group of otherwise independent actors, each acting in pure self-interest, coming together to produce something for the good of all' (Casey and Vigna 2018, p. 12). According to Jesse Walden of Mediachain, a blockchain start-up that has now been acquired by Spotify, the GRD failed because of 'perverse incentives that require participants to cede control of their data to some third party'; blockchain technology, by contrast, means that 'anyone can participate, and each participant retains control over their data' (Howard 2017, pp. 200–201).

To create a successful, decentralised GRD is ambitious, and the challenge is social as well as technological. Yet the potential for networking databases is significant. Consider Blokur, a start-up that 'reduces costs and increases revenue for music publishers and CMOs (collective management organisations) through automation and better data, enabled by blockchain technology and machine learning' (Blokur 2018). Founder Phil Barry elaborates in our interview:

> *O'Dair*: How important is blockchain technology to your value system (i.e. the value chain as it extends beyond your specific company to suppliers, distributors and customers) and why?
>
> *Barry*: Blockchain is important to the connectivity of the value chain because it provides an efficient interaction model for a group of diverse participants. A function of Blokur's decision to use blockchain

technology, therefore, is that the rights value chain looks much more like an ecosystem and less like a linear value chain in terms of data flow.

The opportunity, in other words, lies in distributed creativity. A similar argument is put forward by JAAK, a start-up using blockchain technology to 'allow the music and media industries to collaborate on a global view of content ownership and rights', with the aim of simplifying content licensing through 'smart content' (JAAK 2018). Dan Fowler, Head of Strategy and Operations, suggests in our interview that is where blockchain technology can be transformative:

O'Dair: What do you consider the main benefits that blockchain technology can offer, both to your business and across your industry more broadly?

Fowler: The media industries are underpinned by a complicated rights structure and siloed information. This negatively impacts stakeholders with high supply chain costs and missed revenue opportunities. The industry has converged on a solution in the form of a global view of rights. However, previous centralised attempts to create this have failed, primarily due to the requirement for centralised control and governance, upfront industry-wide consensus, and misaligned incentives. We believe that blockchains and a decentralised approach offer a potential remedy due to their ability to enable 1) a network of participants; 2) to collaboratively maintain a single dataset; 3) without a central authority.

For Fowler, aligning incentives to encourage collaboration is key:

O'Dair: What do you consider the main barriers to adoption, both within your company and beyond, and how might those barriers be overcome? Please consider political, economic, social, technological, legal and/or environmental factors.

Fowler: The complexity of legacy technology, process, and data is a challenge; however, value is also incredibly consolidated, and rights are by their nature very sticky. We are building global infrastructure – a comprehensive network. Thus, any solution that we design needs to work for all rights holders. Balancing these requirements has been insurmountable to date and will require incentive mechanisms that build cooperative pressure. We believe that the best approach to do this is through extensive engagement with, and listening to, the users for whom we are building the network. This enables us to align short-term commercial interests of individual stakeholders with the long-term goals of the industry.

If a blockchain is operated by its stakeholders, the motives of participants are aligned with the goals of the registry (De Filippi et al. 2016, p. 6). Blockchains allow for a system that is politically and architecturally decentralised, in that it is beyond the control of any individual and has no single point of failure, but logically centralised, in that it effectively functions as a single giant computer (Buterin 2017). This more inclusive model would encourage innovation, encouraging start-ups to use that data to build apps and other services.

Distributed Ownership

The notion of the author, as we understand the term today, emerged in parallel with the development of copyright (Saunders 1992; Woodmanmsee and Jaszi 1994) and the increased emphasis on individual genius in the Romantic era (Bennett 2005; Burke 1995; Foucault 1984). Yet the reality is that many creative works do not have a single author. In fact, scholars such as Bilton (2007) and Hartley et al. (2015) have argued that we should understand creativity as not located in the individual 'lone genius' but, rather, in groups and systems. Today, we now have the technology to facilitate creative collaboration on a larger scale than ever before. We do not, however, have the infrastructure to properly remunerate it.

One crucial feature of blockchain technology is its potential to encourage good behaviour between parties who do not know or trust one another. This could incentivise new forms of large-scale decentralised collaboration right across the creative economy, with individuals receiving rewards according to the perceived value of their contribution. For a sense of how this might work, we can turn to Backfeed—an initiative that uses blockchain technology to encourage massive, open-source collaboration between peers without centralised control. 'Backfeed introduces a social protocol on top of blockchain-based infrastructures to coordinate individuals through the creation and distribution of economic tokens and reputation scores so as to eventually allow for the emergence of meritocratic systems and emergent alternative economies' (Davidson et al. 2016, p. 15). The result could be 'massive open-source collaboration without any form of centralised coordination' (Davidson et al. 2016, p. 15). Through transferrable economic tokens and non-transferrable reputation scores, Backfeed aims to become a Decentralised Collaborative Organisation—drawing on open source ideology but applicable not just to software but to numerous fields, including content creation.

We have already seen the Cypherfunks, a group of musicians based all over the world using cryptocurrencies to share ownership of the music they created together (De Filippi et al. 2016, p. 19). Also, UK Games Talent and Finance (UKGTF), a not-for-profit working to improve the early-stage ecosystem for UK video games developers, has developed a new type of IP share—a 'Tal'—as a cost-effective means of tracking the founding creators' shares. In conjunction with Digital Catapult, ULGTF has already run a successful pilot examining the potential of recording transactions on a distributed ledger (Durant and Hogarth 2016). In the future, De Filippi et al. suggest, we might find freelance journalists coming together to form decentralised news collectives, or thousands of writers collaborating on books (Davidson et al. 2016). Consider Civil, a 'decentralised, ethereum-based marketplace that aims to introduce a new, sustainable operating model for journalism' (Civil 2018):

> Civil's cryptoeconomic model seeks to enable a more direct, transparent relationship between journalists and citizens, while using blockchain to also strengthen protections for journalists against censorship and intellectual property violations. The goal of Civil is to create a sustainable, global marketplace for journalism that is free from manipulative ads, misinformation and outside influence. (Civil 2018)

Co-founder Christine Mohan elaborated on Civil's mission in our interview:

O'Dair: How important is blockchain technology to your business model and why? Please consider value proposition; market; operations; and finances.

Mohan: Blockchain technology is critical to our business model of creating a decentralised platform for sustainable journalism. Blockchain enables self-governance (CVL tokens represent ownership in a cooperative network, and also act as voting chips for the community governance model) and permanence (permanent recording of authorship and content, via the blockchain's distributed ledger). The Civil Registry is what makes Civil truly different from other journalism models; we're introducing cryptoeconomic incentives, underpinned by the Civil Constitution, a foundational, 'rules of the road' document for behaviour on Civil, to ensure that rational behaviour scales with the network, and that special interests aren't able to co-opt the platform's governance model. Inclusion in the Civil Registry means that the community has vetted a Newsroom and deemed it as having a credible, journalistic mission. A Newsroom's status on the Civil Registry can be challenged at any time, if it's found to be in serious violation of the Civil Constitution.

Smart, Transparent Payments and Licensing

Licensing

Partially because of the siloed data landscape, licensing content at present is difficult. We live in an era of 'remix culture' (Lessig 2008) and user-generated content (UGC), of 'co-creation' and blurred boundaries between production and consumption (Benkler 2006; Lessig 2008). 'Amateur culture', suggests Lessig (2006), has historically been free of regulation, but this has changed due to digital technologies. Some of these changes have been positive: digital technologies have radically expanded the scope of amateur culture, as manifest for instance in blogs, vlogs and mash-ups. On the flipside, however, Lessig also argues that amateur culture is subject to regulation in a way that it has never been before. Acquiring a 'sync' license to use a song in a big-budget TV show, or even a Youtube video, will typically require sign-off from a number of people—and it is not always easy even to find out who those people are. Social influencers might be willing to pay to license a major label recording for an online video if it were easy and affordable to do so. At present, however, they are deliberately avoiding such songs, as they are likely to get their videos red-flagged. The significant market for low-value, high volume microlicensing has yet to be properly served.

Blockchain technology, suggests Dan Fowler of JAAK in our interview, can have a role in solving the licensing challenge:

> *O'Dair*: What problem is your business attempting to solve?
>
> *Fowler*: Working with key industry stakeholders, we have identified two problems that we believe that blockchain infrastructure could provide solutions to: an aggregated view of copyright – *who owns what*, and scalable licensing solutions – *lowering the barriers to content.*

As Fowler states, blockchain's potential goes beyond individual business models:

> *O'Dair*: How important is blockchain technology to your value system (i.e. the value chain as it extends beyond your specific company to suppliers, distributors and customers) and why?
>
> *Fowler*: Transparent value distribution and decentralised shared infrastructure will reduce the requirement for parallel non-differentiating investment, and incentivise effort and resource towards value-adding services.

> The result of this will be an industry that has reduced friction in licensing and paying creators, lowers barriers to entry for those that want to contribute to the industry, and offers greater opportunities for users to be able to access content.

If the rights status of a creative work was registered on a blockchain, then the conditions for its use and re-use would be visible to all. There is also considerable potential for smart contracts to automate at least some parts of the licensing process. As Howard (2017, p. 141) suggests, creators could set their own, machine-readable, rules determining how their works can be used (see 'increased control' section below). This would encourage the creation of derivative works, for instance through remixing or sampling. Particularly significant here is COALA IP, the Coalition of Automated Legal Applications, who have developed a blockchain-ready protocol for licensing IP. It is true that authorship might change during—and even after—the creation of a work. Yet 'multisignature' functionality, which ensures that no one person can make a unilateral action, could allow changes to be made at a later date if approved by all stakeholders.

Royalty Payments

Although creative goods enjoy copyright protection, the holder of the copyright must enforce it and collect payments for use of the copyrighted good (Caves 2000). Composers and songwriters face a particular challenge—'the lumps of rent are very small, very numerous, and hence feasible to collect only through some cooperative organisation' (Caves 2000, p. 297)—but the problem is by no means exclusive to music. With streaming, the problem is only getting worse: we are moving towards a micropayments economy (Howard 2017, p. 92) and an exponential increase in data, as we move from the one-off payments required for a CD or download purchase to payments for every single listen (Howard 2017, p. 209). Royalty payments, at present, are startlingly inefficient: they can take months or years to reach creators. In a world in which consumers can access content with a single click, this is archaic. The problem is not just that payments are slow: it is also that, by the time royalties arrive, at least one collection society is likely to have taken a cut. (Collection societies, also known as collective management organisations or collective rights organisations, are membership organisations that manage specific rights, such as photocopying or public performance of sound recordings, on behalf of members in a given country [Towse 2010].) This is a problem since many creators do not believe they are receiving just rewards for their work. In music, for instance, a 'value gap' (IFPI 2017) has been identified between high levels of consumption on streaming platforms such as Youtube and low financial returns for creators.

Blockchains could make royalty payments faster: bitcoin payments occur in minutes, and transactions using other cryptocurrencies, such litecoin, are faster still. This could usher in a world in which playing a song automatically triggers a royalty payment via a smart contract (De Filippi et al. 2016, pp. 2–3), although it should be noted, of course, that royalties are not the only means by which creators are paid; musicians and authors, for instance, also receive advances. Blockchain technology is also associated with a lowering of transaction costs (Gupta 2017). This is important in a streaming era characterised by large numbers of low-value payments. Blockchains could facilitate micropayments to creators: a world in which users pay for content as it streams, or in which books are paid for by the paragraph (De Filippi et al. 2016, p. 3). A direct-to-fan 'tip jar' model has also been envisaged, in which fans make micropayments to an artist to access a particular work.

Consider Publica, a company introducing blockchain technology into book publishing. The company is encouraging authors to pre-sell books as 'readable tokens', with the aim of rewarding early supports and receiving funds required to finish writing (Publica 2018). As CEO Josef Marc points out in our interview, smart contracts reduce costs for revenue distribution. The point is also relevant to FilmChain, a start-up using the ethereum blockchain to collect and automatically allocate film revenues. This, the company states, 'lowers friction, increases transparency and cuts down settlement times' (FilmChain 2018). Co-founders Irina Albita and Maria Tanjala, and community and content manager Jamie Sly, explain how it works in our interview:

O'Dair: Which blockchain are you using and how are you using it (i.e. what is in the blocks and what is off-chain, public or private)?

Albita et al.: FilmChain is a platform for revenue collection and allocation and utilises the ethereum blockchain. FilmChain uses ethereum blockchain in order to increase transparency in the film and digital industries, utilising smart contracts to cut down on settlement times and decrease costs for everyone invested: financiers, equity investors,

> producers, crews, cast, etc. The prototype focuses on the optimisation of business processes and allows independent filmmakers access revenues instantly. When new revenue appears, a proprietary network of smart contracts automatically allocates tokens based on our algorithm, removing the need for a middleman. Stakeholders log onto their dashboards and can withdraw the amounts in their wallets, paid in fiat. The use of blockchain also allows a fully transparent ledger of transactions for the producers, who can verify the incomes of their projects. The platform has different layers of privacy that enables each stakeholder to track their own income streams. The dashboards also provide revenue analyses to empower producers to make informed decisions over marketing spent, for future investment decisions, audiences tracking etc.

Using blockchain technology in this way, Albita et al. argue, can be radically disruptive, in part because it allows for the automation of revenue collection and distribution:

> *O'Dair*: What do you consider the main benefits that blockchain technology can offer, both to your business and across your industry more broadly?
>
> *Albita et al.*: Blockchain technology is a game changer when it comes to the screen industry. Smart contracts have the potential to disrupt various roles within the sector as they allow agreements to be automatically validated, signed and executed by utilising the blockchain ledger. This is important because it removes the need for a middleman and the high fees they charge. Blockchain technology is also useful due to the transparency of the system, allowing individuals to track incoming revenues and how the money was split amongst film stakeholders or digital content creators. Blockchain is useful in tracking ownership, recording digital assets and avoiding ownership disputes.

One possible consequence is disintermediation, removing intermediaries from the value system so that royalty payments could be paid, almost instantaneously, according to agreed percentages. For some, the most obvious impact will be on copyright collection societies. At present, the existence of collection societies means that 'an entire repertoire, comprising all the works by every member of the organisation, is included in a single license by a national collecting society' (Towse 2010, p. 359). Howard (2017, pp. 75, 190) has suggested that blockchain technology will remove societies entirely, since tokens could incentivise good behaviour without any trusted third parties. Such a scenario is not without its risks, however, as I argue in Chapter 5.

Blockchain technology is unlikely to completely remove intermediaries. Instead, adoption might see collection societies, for instance, changing their role, serving as accreditors of metadata while the collection and distribution of royalties is dealt with by smart contracts. Blockchains may also create new intermediaries (Mougayar 2016; O'Dwyer 2017). At least partial disintermediation is possible, however. Consider Maecenas Fine Art, a start-up that uses blockchain technology to democratise investment in visual art:

> By connecting artists, collectors and investors directly via an open blockchain platform with smart contracts, we eliminate the need for brokers and art dealers to facilitate a transaction. We replace the need for trust based on reputation with trust in the decentralised blockchain… By tokenising art, the platform converts million-dollar artworks into smaller financial units that can be bought and sold easily globally through a transparent marketplace. This provides investors with liquidity and a much- needed market-driven price discovery mechanism. (Maecenas 2017)

Transparency

Opacity is a problem in the creative economy, both in the value chains of individual firms and more broadly, across what Porter (1985) refers to as value systems. Royalty payments can lack transparency; so too can supply chains, since they are composed of distinct, independent businesses. Although their interests align around the goal of maximising the sale of an end product, these businesses 'are also engaged in price-sensitive purchasing contracts with each other,' so there is 'an inherent misalignment of interests between different upstream and downstream members of the chain' (Casey and Vigna 2018, pp. 141–142). The result is that, rather than sharing data, each party maintains its own data records.

Blockchains, by contrast, introduce transparency, as Maecenas Fine Art CEO Marcelo Garcia Casil suggests in the interview I conducted for this book:

> *O'Dair*: What do you consider the main benefits that blockchain technology can offer, both to your business and across your industry more broadly?
>
> *Casil*: Blockchain technology offers multiple improvements in efficiency to an industry that has traditionally depended on solely manual processes.

> Art sales information has been notoriously opaque or privy to only a handful of selected experts due to the private nature of many sales. This information asymmetry makes it difficult for interested new investors to break into the art market. Blockchain can provide an open and transparent database of provenance for global artworks, it keeps a record of all transactions when art shares are bought and sold, thus maintaining a reliable pricing record for the art industry.

Blockchain technology, as Blokur's Phil Barry states in our interview, creates an audit trail, for instance of music rights ownership and usage over time. The transparency argument is also made by GUTS, a company using blockchain technology to tackle ticket fraud and the inflated prices in the secondary ticket market—while offering 'absolute transparency for all users' (GET 2017). Olivier Biggs, Communication and Community Manager at GUTS, elaborates in our interview:

O'Dair: How important is blockchain technology to your value system (i.e. the value chain as it extends beyond your specific company to suppliers, distributors and customers) and why?

Biggs: It is a crucial part, as it finally provides transparency in the value chain, exposing the third parties that are now profiting from being able to act 'in the dark', so to speak. This allows them to, for example, easily buy up hundreds or thousands of tickets for a popular concert and sell these tickets back to fans for profit without having to account for their actions. An innovative application of blockchain technology sheds a light on this process and shows who is profiting and when, providing easier ways of restructuring the value chain so the right actors receive the fair rewards.

Transparency, for Biggs, is fundamental:

O'Dair: What do you consider the main benefits that blockchain technology can offer, both to your business and across your industry more broadly?

Biggs: Transparency. It means that transactions are now publicly traceable and all actors involved can be held accountable for their actions. In the case of ticketing this means that no more fraudulent or opportunistic third parties can wedge themselves in between an event organiser and an event attendee to hold the tickets hostage for profit.

The notion of transparency can create confusion, since blockchain technology is associated with privacy. In fact, bitcoin is not all that private, which is why we have seen the emergence of other, more anonymous cryptocurrencies, such as zcash. Users of bitcoin are pseudonymous, rather than anonymous: 'while not explicitly tied to real-world individuals or organisations, all transactions are completely transparent' (Meiklejohn et al. 2013, p. 1). This mix of pseudonymity and transparency could be brought to the creative economy. Blockchains could bring transparency to revenue payments, Tapscott and Tapscott (2018, p. 233) suggest, making accounting and auditing more efficient. At the same time, Christine Mohan states in our interview that journalists might benefit from the privacy and pseudonymity offered by blockchain technology. Another area of concern, here, is that commercially sensitive data would become visible to all. This, however, is to ignore the existence of permissioned, as well as permissionless, systems. It is also to neglect the existence of zero-knowledge proofs: the ability 'to prove without revealing' (Quisquater et al. 1990, p. 630). The key point is that blockchains can offer *selective* transparency: they can be as transparent as their users desire (De Filippi et al. 2016, p. 5). Artists and managers could see whether payments were being efficiently processed, for example, without making that data available to the general public.

In the case of supply chains, meanwhile, companies that do not currently share information could use hashes to verify that key procedures had taken place without revealing any secret information. 'Those hashes can then be recorded into a blockchain to which all chain members have access, creating an easily traceable, immutable record to which all have consented, one that naturally enhances trust in the data' (Casey and Vigna 2018, p. 142).

Providing physical assets are made uniquely identifiable, for instance through watermarking, a blockchain can be used to securely track objects along a supply chain; the ledger can then be 'signed' upon receipt of goods (Elsden et al. 2018, p. 6).

Increased Control

Setting Parameters for Pricing and Using Creative Works

At present, most creators do not set prices for their works. Collection societies set the prices for licensing, for instance, while the British singer, songwriter, musician and producer Imogen Heap has noted that she does not have the right to release music for free, should she want to, on specific days of the year such as her birthday. Since artists 'cannot feasibly select where, when and how their music is publicly performed', an artist might, for instance, find one of her songs being used by a politician with whom she strongly disagrees (Howard 2017, p. 237).

Howard (2017, p. 22) states that, as well as registering their works on a blockchain, creators could register associated 'rules':

> In this manner, the original creator would not only be on record as the creator but – utilising smart contracts – also determine how /if /when / and at what price their works could be used by others, and be compensated – financially or via smart contracts – when such use took place. (Howard 2017, p. 23)

Tapscott and Tapscott (2018, p. 234) suggest that blockchains could allow for dynamic pricing: an advertiser who has licensed a song for a commercial could be required to pay more for that license if there is a spike in that song's downloads or streams. Howard (2017, pp. 240–241) also points to the possibility of 'dynamic pricing', so creators would be able to change pricing to reflect demand in much the same way that Uber changes its fares.

Certainly, blockchain technology could be used to bring control to creators: artists could choose, for instance, whether or not to allow adverts to interrupt the streaming of their songs (Tapscott and Tapscott 2018, p. 234). Publica allows authors to set the token price for their projects (Publica 2018). Howard (2017, p. 233) suggests that a creator might allow fans to use a song in the background for a social media video, but automatically demand an additional payment if that video achieved a certain number of likes or shares. Howard also states that an artist could also refuse to allow their music to be used during political events (p. 238). As I argue in Chapter 5, however, there is also a risk in this increased individualisation, particularly in relation to blanket licensing.

Setting Parameters for Pricing and Using Tickets

The current challenge for ticketing—an issue relevant to all performing arts—is effectively outlined in the GET white paper:

> Ticket fraud and exorbitant secondary ticket prices are age old phenomena that have had artists and their fans worried since the times of Dickens and Shakespeare. Thirty percent of all tickets are resold with mark-ups between 30% and 700%. The ticket market is non-transparent, and inexplicable transaction costs added to tickets are common practice among ticketing companies. (GET 2017)

For GUTS, blockchain technology—specifically the Guaranteed Entrance Token (GET)—offers a solution to this problem:

> The solution is a blockchain based event ticketing protocol that will make exorbitant secondary market ticket prices and ticket fraud occurrences of the past. The protocol will offer these features while providing absolute transparency for all users. This goal will be reached by introducing a smart-ticketing protocol built upon the ethereum blockchain that will facilitate the sale of event tickets by issuing smart tickets to wallet addresses on the blockchain. The owner of a smart ticket is free to sell his or her ticket but has to do so within the decentralised infrastructure of the protocol. This ensures that trades are done safely and within a strict price margin bound. (GET 2017)

Artos, a company that presents itself as 'the bridge to blockchain for the ticketing industry' (Artos 2018), are operating in a similar space, as Chief Technology Officer Andy Grant explains in our interview:

> *O'Dair*: What problem is your business attempting to solve?
> *Grant*: The Aventus Protocol has been developed to revolutionise the ticketing industry by giving ticketing rights holders greater control and security over inventory pricing and transactions. This will virtually eliminate ticketing fraud and unregulated, unethical touting activities.

Artos deploy the blockchain-based event ticketing protocol developed by Aventus, one advantage of which is that event organisers can set (and enforce) minimum and maximum resale prices for tickets:

> Aventus is a global open standard for the exchange of tickets. Its blockchain-based platform eliminates uncontrolled resale and counterfeit tickets. It allows event organisers to create, manage and promote their events and tickets with dramatically reduced costs, even letting them set price controls and receive commissions on ticket resales. It also gives ticket buyers rewards for promoting events, and identifying fraudulent activity. (Vey and Monari 2017)

New Business Models

Consumption Data

Data, it is said, is new oil. Information about the streaming, liking, and sharing of work by fans is extremely valuable: according to O'Dwyer (2017, p. 303), it may be more valuable than the artist's work in generating additional revenue streams. Artists should be able to leverage that data, for instance to attract sponsors or plan tours (O'Dwyer 2017, p. 304). At present, however, this valuable data about the consumption of artists' work is held by intermediaries, rather than artists themselves (Heap 2017). There is, in other words, significant information asymmetry.

Blockchain technology could facilitate 'a possible shift in the monetisation of culture from the sale and production of scarce goods toward artists instead financialising data associated with their use and circulation' (O'Dwyer 2017, p. 304):

> *Digital culture wants to be free in the world of blockchains*, not because the blockchain is a democratic tool that will abolish the exploitation of artists by big business but because stronger property rights and legalities are no longer where the money is at. (O'Dwyer 2017, p. 307, emphasis in original)

The possibility, then, is not necessarily in selling creative works in larger quantities; instead, it lies in 'the potentially richer information that would be widely available once an immutable link to the musicians makes a file traceable' (Casey and Vigna 2018, pp. 233–234). As Blokur founder Phil Barry states in our interview, this could bring about the end of silos:

O'Dair: What do you consider the main benefits that blockchain technology can offer, both to your business and across your industry more broadly?

Barry: The opportunity for Blokur is to use blockchain technology to underpin a new model for multi-party interactions that solves our customers' data problems. More broadly, blockchain technology is a shared infrastructure that allows data and automation to live outside of a traditional corporate structure, which represents a big leap forward in terms of efficiency and co-ordination.

Data is also a critical issue for Maecenas CEO Marcelo Garcia Casil; as he states in our interview, their users appreciate access to market data in order to make informed decisions about how to best manage their investments.

Digital Scarcity

Digitisation has made copying easier and cheaper—and, unlike analogue copies, 'the quality of digital reproduction is near flawless' (Klein et al. 2015, p. 17). This is a particular problem given that the creative industries are characterised by high production costs and low reproduction costs, and that users are inclined to share products freely, regarding them as public goods (Klein et al. 2015, pp. 28–30):

> In sum, digitisation has made unauthorised access and distribution of copyrighted work easy and ordinary which, in turn, has provided a catalyst to conversations not simply about how to enforce copyright and punish transgression, but whether copyright, as it is currently understood and regulated, is the right way to encourage and reward creative expression. (Klein et al. 2015, p. 3)

Blockchain technology introduces digital scarcity: 'contrary to the infinitely copiable world of plenty we associate with digital media, the blockchain makes finitude and singularity possible' (Dodd 2017, p. 17). The problem with digital files, after all, is in essence a 'double spend' problem—precisely the problem that bitcoin was designed to solve (McAfee and Brynjolfsson 2017, p. 281). Digital scarcity could result in the introduction of digital collectibles: unique and non-fungible (not easily exchanged for similar items) digital assets. The non-fungible aspect is key, and marks a key distinction from cryptocurrencies: while currencies have to be fungible, or mutually interchangeable, every collectible must be different. The phenomenon of Rare Pepes—images based on Pepe the Frog and treated as digital trading cards—was an early example of this trend. As Fred Wilson of Union Square Ventures has pointed out, Rare Pepes come with alt-right associations that many will find deeply off-putting; they are also somewhat clunky to use. At the same time, Wilson notes the considerable potential:

> So why do I think this is interesting? Well for one, it shows the utility of a blockchain in action. You can buy, sell, hold, and transfer digital assets and they have value and are traded for other digital assets (like BTC [bitcoin]) in an online global marketplace. Anyone can make one of these cards and if they are determined to be 'rare' they become digital assets with value attached to them. It also shows how a game can be built on a blockchain with virtual goods and characters and more. (Wilson 2017)

Since Rare Pepes, other cryptocollectibles have been announced, including Leci Gou and Hash Puppies (variations based on dogs) and CryptoFighters (a variation based on warriors). The most significant cryptocollectible, however, has been CryptoKitties: 'digital, collectible cats built on the ethereum blockchain' (CryptoKitties 2017). CryptoKitties can be bought and sold using ether, and cats can even 'breed' to create new cats which users can then trade on ethereum. Digital scarcity, as Schwab (2016, p.155) states, could bring about 'an explosion in tradable assets'. CryptoKitties, promoted with a pun-filled white paper (or 'white pa-purr'), are sometimes seen as a lightweight blockchain application but the potential of cryptocollectibles is considerable—and the project was explicitly intended as 'practical experimentation and application of digital scarcity, digital collectibles, and non-fungible tokens' (CryptoKitties 2017). As Bryce Bladon states in our interview for this book, CryptoKitties was designed to meet three main aims:

> *O'Dair*: What problem is your business attempting to solve?
> *Bladon*: – Show a consumer case for blockchain technology
> – Showcase a non-cryptocurrency application for blockchain technology
> – Dispel myths and help educate the world on the wider implications of blockchain technology.

The benefit of blockchain technology, as Bladon points out during the interview, lies in at least partial disintermediation: blockchains facilitate peer-to-peer transactions without a trusted third party.

Smart droit de suite *Payments*

Some jurisdictions recognise *droit de suite*, the right for artists or their heirs to receive a fee upon the resale of their works. This right is not recognised in all countries, however, and artists and their heirs cannot, in any case, keep track of their works as they change hands. As a result, many artists only receive payment when a work of art is first sold. This is not only a problem in the art world, but in other creative industries too: a novelist, for instance, collects every time her book is sold, although not every time it is read (Caves 2000, p. 313), and there is no money for the author if the book is re-sold.

Blockchain technology reduces transaction costs and, in automating payments, brings speed we well as selective transparency to payments. These advantages are outlined in more detail in the 'royalty payments' section above. In terms of *droit de suite*, however, the advantages go beyond efficiency to introducing a new revenue stream—and, therefore, changing business models. Consider Publica, a company using blockchain technology to offer authors the chance to receive a portion of the resale price of their books (Publica 2018). As CEO Josef Marc states in our interview, there is potential here for a new type of secondary market for digital books, with authors being part a portion of re-sale revenue though smart contracts. A similar model is emerging in visual art, with smart contracts allowing artists—and, in some cases, other stakeholders—to be paid every time an artwork is sold or re-sold. For instance, Artlery, a company that describes itself as a 'a next generation artist rights and equity platform', guarantees automatic payments to all stakeholders—a gallery, a curator, any patrons—as well as guaranteeing direct payments to the relevant artist every time an artwork is resold (Artlery 2018). Although it would not fall under *droit de suite*, the concept is broadly similar to that proposed by Aventus, where event organsiers can receive a portion of revenue from ticket sales on secondary markets (Vey and Morari 2017).

Tokens

Start-ups, particularly those without a track record, face challenges in attracting finance, in part due to information asymmetries. Information asymmetries may be a particular challenge for innovative and creative new ventures, since they are especially difficult for investors to understand. Another challenge is that many new ventures in the creative economy require relatively small amounts of money, which for some investors do not justify the process of due diligence. The result is a financing gap, which angel investment can only partially overcome. Reward-model crowdfunding, in which funders receive a pre-determined product or service in return for a financial contribution, has not proved a sustainable alternative either: even creators who have run successful campaigns have found them difficult to repeat, given the danger of 'going to the well one too many times' (Davidson and Poor 2015). As a result, the do-it-yourself potential of the digital era has not been realised: traditional intermediaries, able to offer advances, retain market dominance.

Through selling tokens to early backers in so-called ICOs, blockchain start-ups can unlock new sources of capital (Swan 2015, p. 12). Smart contracts bring reliability to the crowdfunding process. If creators reach their funding objectives, they receive the pledged funds; if they do not, the money is returned to funders. Again, then, blockchain technology could remove parties from the value system.

The ICO acronym deliberately echoes the initial public offering (IPO), yet token sales, unlike IPOs, often do not typically offer equity-like value. In fact, tokens vary wildly: 'Some tokens are similar to currencies, others are more like securities, and others have properties that are entirely new' (Conley 2017, p. 1). IPOs are also highly regulated, while token sales face considerable legal and regulatory uncertainty. Still, the impact of token sales as a means of raising capital is considerable, with billions of dollars raised to date, often at astonishing speeds: $35 million in 35 seconds is not unheard of, even for companies yet to produce a product (Sahdev 2017). During a two-month period in 2017, a total of $830 million was raised, via token sales, by just four companies: Filecoin, Bancor, Texos and EOS (Casey and Vigna 2018, p. 105). $5.6 billion was apparently raised via token sales in 2017; at the time of writing, in June 2018, the total raised via token sales this year is reportedly close to $10.5 billion.

As regards creative economy examples, Singular DTV, a blockchain entertainment studio, rights management platform and Transactional Video on Demand portal, raised $7.5 million (or its equivalent in ether) via a token sale in 2017. Also in 2017, TRON, a project that aims to use blockchain technology to construct a new kind of content entertainment system, raised the equivalent of $70 million.

Among the respondents I interviewed for this book, Civil are planning a token sale, while Aventus have already held one. It is notable, however, that many blockchain start-ups are *not* funded by token sales; CryptoKitties, for instance, received funding from VCs such as Andreessen Horowitz and Union Square Ventures, as Bryce Bladon states in our interview; it is actually stated in the CryptoKitties white paper that they are seeking a more sustainable revenue model than a one-off token sale (CryptoKitties 2017). This revenue model is outlined by Bladon in our interview:

> *O'Dair*: [How important is blockchain technology to your] finances (i.e. your revenue streams and cost structure)?
>
> *Bladon*: Outside of partnerships and special auctions, we make 3.75% of each sale conducted on our marketplace and 100% of the proceeds of 'Gen 0' cats, which are released every fifteen minutes for the first year of our product's life.

Publica CEO Josef Marc outlines a broadly similar model for his company in our interview, with Publica retaining 10% of PBL transactions, or book sales. Maecenas, meanwhile, charge a fee for each successful transaction. CEO Marcelo Garcia Casil elaborates in the interview conducted for this book:

> *O'Dair*: [How important is blockchain technology to your] finances (i.e. your revenue streams and cost structure)?
>
> *Casil*: Maecenas plays the role of marketplace and 'matchmaker' for fine art sellers and buyers. We charge a small fee of 2% to buyers and 6% to sellers for each successful transaction. This is much lower than the current margins charged by galleries and auction houses that can be as high as 25% of the sale price. The historically high commission rates reflect the current monopoly of trust held by these longstanding institutions – trust that can be democratised with the use of the blockchain to increase transparency. We will be accepting both fiat and cryptocurrencies on the platform, which will be converted into our own utility token, ART, which will act as a base currency for clearing and also necessary for the technology and smart contracts to run.

For any blockchain start-up, token sales are a tempting means to access alternative sources of finance. To have long-term value, however, these tokens (be they ERC20, as used, for instance, by Publica, or ERC-721, as pioneered by CryptoKitties) require *utility*. Creators can issue specific benefits to patrons, such as backstage access, previews of new works or a share of profits. This is about new customer relationships, in other words, not simply new revenue streams. The potential of blockchain technology lies in distributed creativity: think of Imogen Heap, for instance, allowing fans to access the 'stems' (individual instrumental and vocal parts) of 'Tiny Human', the song she released using the ethereum blockchain in 2015, in order to create their own remixes. Such moves represent an enormous boost to distributed creativity—and, thanks to blockchain technology, all derivative works can point back to the original, known by Heap, in a reference to the 'genesis block' on the bitcoin blockchain, as the 'genesis work' (Howard 2017, p. 48).

Conclusion

For the creative economy, blockchain technology offers very significant opportunities. It could make it much easier for creators to claim ownership of their works, as well as to share that ownership; it could also allow ownership data to be stored in a decentralised, but logically centralised, database, bringing an end to discrete data silos. Royalty payments and licensing can become automated, via smart contracts; payments can also become at least selectively transparent. Creators could gain additional control over the prices charged for their work and the types of usage permitted; event promoters, too, can gain control over ticket re-sales. Finally, new business models could become possible, with creators benefitting from access to consumption data that is currently captured by intermediaries; from digital scarcity and the introduction of cryptocollectibles; from automated *droit de suite* or re-sale payments; and, finally, from tokens. Tokens are most effective, however, when they are understood as linked to a company's entire business model, not simply a source of start-up capital. To understand the full potential of tokens, in fact, it is necessary to think beyond the individual company altogether to the overall value system. This is suggested in the interview I conducted with Irina Albita, Maria Tanjala, and Jamie Sly of FilmChain:

O'Dair: How important is blockchain technology to your value system (i.e. the value chain as it extends beyond your specific company to suppliers, distributors and customers) and why?

Albita et al.: The film value chain is determined by several stages: financing, development, production, post-production, sale, distribution and exhibition. Throughout all these stages, a new business model, powered by blockchain technology, is making a strong move. Integrated solutions from financing to exhibition are taking shape. The encompassing vision for blockchain solutions is to enable, at the point of the content consumption, a real-time allocation of revenues with anyone that has worked on a project. Our only reservation at the moment is around the financing stage – where, in an unclear regulatory landscape, financing films though Initial Token/Coin Offerings is not yet a viable solution. Currently, FilmChain is taking a realistic step-by-step development approach, working within the boundaries of the current film business model to present a real alternative to collection services and real-time monitoring of revenues.

The lack of regulatory clarity is indeed a significant barrier to adoption—one of a number I examine in the following chapter.

References

Artley. 2018. https://artlery.com/artists. Accessed 25 June 2018.

Artos. 2018. https://www.artos.io. Accessed 21 June 2018.

Bazalgette, P. 2017. Independent Review of the Creative Industries. https://assets.publishing.service.gov.uk/government/uploads/system/uploads/attachment_data/file/649980/Independent_Review_of_the_Creative_Industries.pdf. Accessed 2 May 2017.

Benkler, Y. 2006. *The Wealth of Networks: How Social Production Transforms Markets and Freedom*. New Haven and London: Yale University Press.

Bennett, A. 2005. *The Author*. Abingdon and New York: Routledge.

Bilton, C. 2007. *Management and Creativity: From Creative Industries to Creative Management*. Oxford: Blackwell.

Blokur. 2018. https://www.blokur.com. Accessed 21 June 2018.

Burke, S. 1995. *Authorship: From Plato to the Postmodern*. Edinburgh: Edinburgh University Press.

Buterin, V. 2017. The Meaning of Decentralization. *Medium*. https://medium.com/@VitalikButerin/the-meaning-of-decentralization-a0c92b76a274. Accessed 16 September 2017.

Casey, M., and P. Vigna. 2018. *The Truth Machine: The Blockchain and the Future of Everything*. London: Harper Collins.
Caves, R. 2000. *Creative Industries: Contracts Between Art and Commerce*. Cambridge, MA: Harvard University Press.
Civil. 2018. White Paper. https://civil.co/white-paper/. Accessed 21 June 2018.
Conley, J. 2017. Blockchain and the Economics of Crypto-Tokens and Initial Coin Offerings. Vanderbilt University Department of Economics Working Paper Series. http://www.accessecon.com/Pubs/VUECON/VUECON-17-00008.pdf. Accessed 10 November 2017.
CryptoKitties. 2017. Collectible and Breedable Cats Empowered by Blockchain Technology. White Pa-Purr Version 2.0. https://drive.google.com/file/d/1soo-eAaJHzhw_XhFGMJp3VNcQoM43byS/view. Accessed 21 June 2018.
Davidson, R., and N. Poor. 2015. The Barriers Facing Artists' Use of Crowdfunding Platforms: Personality, Emotional Labor, and Going to the Well One Too Many Times. *New Media and Society* 17 (2): 289–307.
Davidson, S., P. De Filippi, and J. Potts. 2016. Economics of Blockchain. https://ssrn.com/abstract=2744751. Accessed 25 August 2017.
De Filippi, P., and A. Wright. 2018. *Blockchain and the Law: The Rule of Code*. Cambridge, MA: Harvard University Press.
De Filippi, P., G. McMullen, T. McConaghy, C. Choi, S. de la Rouviere, J. Benet, and D. Stern. 2016. How Blockchains Can Support, Complement, or Supplement Intellectual Property: Working Draft, Version 1.0, COALA. http://docplayer.net/56177308-How-blockchains-can-support-complement-or-supplement-intellectual-property.html. Accessed 4 May 2018.
Dodd, N. 2017. The Social Life of Bitcoin. *Theory, Culture and Society* 35: 35–56.
Durant, P., and M. Hogarth. 2016. Tal Stories: A New Concept for Creative Teams to Share Project Ownership and Revenues. UK Games Talent and Finance.
Elsden, C., A. Manohar, J. Briggs, M. Harding, C. Speed, and J. Vines. 2018. Making Sense of Blockchain Applications: A Typology for HCI. In *Proceedings of the 2018 CHI Conference*, 21–26 April, Montreal. https://chriselsden.files.wordpress.com/2018/01/elsden-making-sense-of-blockchain-applications.pdf. Accessed 4 May 2018.
Filmchain. 2018. http://filmchain.co. Accessed 21 June 2018.
Foucault, M. 1984. What Is an Author? In *The Foucault Reader: An Introduction to Foucault's Thought*, ed P. Rainbow, 101–120. Penguin: London.
GET. 2017. White Paper. https://guts.tickets/files/GET-Whitepaper-GUTS-Tickets-latest.pdf. Accessed 22 June 2018.
Gupta, V. 2017. A Brief History of Blockchain. *Harvard Business Review*. https://hbr.org/2017/02/a-brief-history-ofblockchain. Accessed 10 November 2017.

Hartley, J., W. Wen, and H. Li. 2015. *Creative Economy and Culture: Challenges, Changes and Futures for the Creative Industries*. London: Sage.
Heap, I. 2017. Blockchain Could Help Musicians Make Money Again. *Harvard Business Review*. https://hbr.org/2017/06/blockchain-could-help-musicians-make-money-again. Accessed 24 October 2017.
Howard, G. 2017. *Everything in Its Right Place: How Blockchain Technology Will Lead to a More Transparent Music Industry*. Beverly Farms, MA: 9GiantSteps.
IFPI. 2017. Global Music Report 2017. http://www.ifpi.org/downloads/GMR2017.pdf. Accessed 10 November 2017.
JAAK. 2018. https://jaak.io. Accessed 22 June 2018.
Klein, B., G. Moss, and L. Edwards. 2015. *Understanding Copyright: Intellectual Property in the Digital Age*. London: Sage.
Lessig, L. 2006. *Code Version 2.0*. New York: Basic Books.
Lessig, L. 2008. *Remix: Making Art and Commerce Thrive in the Hybrid Economy*. London: Bloomsbury.
Maecenas. 2017. White Paper. https://www.maecenas.co/Maecenas-WhitePaper.pdf. Accessed 21 June 2018.
McAfee, A., and E. Brynjolfsson. 2017. *Machine Platform Crowd: Harnessing Our Digital Future*. New York and London: Norton.
Meiklejohn, S., M. Pomarole, G. Jordan, K. Levchenko, D. McCoy, G. Voelker, and S. Savage. 2013. A Fistful of Bitcoins: Characterising Payments Among Men with No Names. *Proceedings of the 2013 Internet Measurement Conference*, ACM, 127–140, Barcelona, Spain.
Mougayar, W. 2016. *The Business Blockchain: Promise, Practice and Application of the Next Internet Technology*. Hoboken: Wiley.
O'Dwyer, R. 2017. Does Digital Culture Want to Be Free? How Blockchains Are Transforming the Economy of Cultural Goods. In *Artists Re:Thinking the Blockchain*, ed. R. Catlow, M. Garrett, N. Jones, and S. Skinner. Liverpool: Liverpool University Press.
Porter, M. 1985. *Competitive Advantage: Creating and Sustaining Superior Performance*. New York: Free Press.
Publica. 2018. https://publica.com. Accessed 21 June 2018.
Quisquater, J., M. Quisquater, M. Quisquater, M. Quisquater, L. Guillou, M. Guillou, G. Guillou, A. Guillou, G. Guillou, S. Guillou, and T. Berson. 1990. How to Explain Zero-Knowledge Protocols to Your Children. Advances in Cryptology—CRYPTO '89, ed. G. Brassard, 628–631. Lecture Notes in Computer Science No. 435. New York: Springer.
Sahdev, N. 2017. The Tokenization of the Economy: ICOs and the Implications for Cryptoeconomics. https://ssrn.com/abstract=3057083. Accessed 10 November 2017.
Saunders, D. 1992. *Authorship and Copyright*. London and New York: Routledge.

Schwab, K. 2016. *The Fourth Industrial Revolution*. London: Portfolio Penguin.
Swan, M. 2015. *Blockchain: Blueprint for a New Economy*. Beijing: O'Reilly.
Tapscott D., and A. Tapscott. 2018. *Blockchain Revolution: How the Technology Behind Bitcoin and Other Cryptocurrencies Is Changing the World*, updated edition. New York: Penguin Random House.
Towse, R. 2010. *A Textbook of Cultural Economics*. Cambridge: Cambridge University Press.
Verisart. 2018. https://www.verisart.com. Accessed 21 June 2018.
Vey, A., and A. Monari. 2017. Aventus White Paper, Version 3. https://aventus.io/doc/whitepaper.pdf. Accessed 22 June 2018.
Walport, M. (ed.). 2016. *Distributed Ledger Technology: Beyond Blockchain*. London: Wordlink. www.gov.uk/government/uploads/system/uploads/attachment_data/file/492972/gs-16-1-distributed-ledger-technology.pdf. Accessed 3 February 2016.
Wilson, F. 2017. Rare Pepe. https://avc.com/2017/05/rare-pepe/. Accessed 21 June 2018.
Woodmansee, M., and P. Jaszi (eds.). 1994. *The Construction of Authorship: Textual Appropriation in Law and Literature*. Durham: Duke University Press.

CHAPTER 4

Barriers to Adoption

Abstract Blockchain technology may have the potential to transform the creative economy but there are a number of barriers to adoption. As regards *political* barriers, politicians and policy-makers are inconsistent in their treatment of blockchain technology, especially in relation to tokens; many governments have yet to clearly articulate their positions. This is off-putting to some potential enterprise users, and hinders the development of standards. As regards *economic* barriers, disruptive/radical applications are likely to be resisted by incumbents, although some incumbents are certainly exploring incorporative/sustaining applications. Even disruptive/radical applications may not be as radical as some proponents claim, due to the impossibility of writing complete contracts. In terms of *social* barriers, the adoption of cryptocurrencies is still relatively low; widespread adoption of blockchain technology is likely to depend on accessibility to users who do not own cryptocurrencies, and who may not be aware that they are using blockchains at all. In terms of *technological* barriers, scalability, in particular, is a significant concern. And while blockchain technology may be groundbreaking, the 'garbage in/garbage out' problem remains—as does the problem of 'breaking the chain'. As regards *legal* barriers, cryptocurrencies and tokens exist in a grey area; there is particular uncertainty over which tokens do, and do not, qualify as securities. Finally, there are *environmental* barriers, due to the energy-intensive nature of achieving proof-of-work consensus.

M. O'Dair, *Distributed Creativity*,
https://doi.org/10.1007/978-3-030-00190-2_4

Keywords Blockchain policy · Blockchain economics · Blockchains and society · Blockchain scalability · Blockchain law · Blockchains and the environment

In the previous chapter, I outlined twelve opportunities for the creative economy in adopting blockchain technology. There are two important caveats, however. The first is that the technology is immature: significant barriers to adoption remain, most obviously in terms of scalability. The second caveat is that there also exist barriers to adoption that have nothing directly to do with the technology itself. To examine any technology in isolation, in fact, is to fall prey to technological determinism: if the best technology always won out then, prior to DVDs and streaming, we would all have been watching films on Betamax rather than on VHS. I analyse barriers to adoption below, utilising the PESTLE framework to divide those barriers into political, economic, social, technological, legal and environmental factors.

Political

Governments intervene in communication, media and cultural markets in three main ways: they *legislate* by creating laws; they *subsidise*, both directly (theatre, ballet, opera, fine art) and indirectly (taking knowledge from the public sector into the private sector); and they *regulate*, creating agencies that monitor an industry or group of industries (Hesmondhalgh 2007, p. 106). Legislation is dealt with in the 'Legal' section below. Direct subsidy of particular art forms is not particularly relevant here, although policy-makers can certainly help remove barriers to adoption through indirect subsidies, for instance to promote research and development (Bakhshi and Lomas 2017). I focus here, then, on regulation.

Regulation gets a bad name among bitcoin users (Narayanan et al. 2016, p. 183). Yet it seems inevitable that governments will take an interest in blockchain technology, given their obligation to maintain capital controls and to prevent money laundering, kidnapping, extortion and tax evasion, all of which can be carried out using cryptocurrencies (Narayanan et al. 2016, pp. 178–179), even if the criminal potential is sometimes overstated—particularly when compared to cash. In practice, many would welcome increased blockchain regulation, particularly of tokens and token sales (PWC 2017). The lack of token regulation to date has served to encourage scams and fraudsters (Guadamaz and Marsden 2015, p. 12). Some start-ups are actively working with regulators, as Bryce Bladon, founding team member at CryptoKitties, states in our interview:

> *O'Dair*: What one step could policy-makers take to promote the adoption of blockchain technology in the creative industries in what you would consider a positive manner?
>
> *Bladon*: CryptoKitties worked with local regulators prior to launching. Though it was time-consuming, it was a process that benefitted both parties and ensured the best possible scenario for consumers. Be proactive and make education a central feature for all parties involved.

Regulation should be encouraged where necessary, then, but it will require caution and precision (Kiviat 2015):

> Governments can send the wrong signals to the market, to policy makers, and to law enforcement agencies, who are typically proxies to them. In addition, heavy-handed government actions risk short-circuiting the private sector leadership in blockchain technology, which is known to bear the fruit of innovation. Of course, government regulation may be applicable for consumer protection and certain other level of standards, but early interference will generally not be helpful. (Mougayar 2016, p. 78)

While the regulation of a permissioned ledger is relatively straightforward, regulating an unpermissioned ledger is challenging to say the least (Lehdonvirta and Ali 2016). Regulating a cryptocurrency such as bitcoin may be almost impossible—and even if it *were* possible, it is likely that another cryptocurrency would simply take its place (Kaplanov 2012, p. 167). There is no doubt that blockchain technology makes it harder to regulate individual behaviour through national laws and regulations; it is difficult to see how governments could control a DAO, for instance (Wright and De Filippi 2015).

It is possible, of course, to regulate the intermediaries, such as exchanges and wallet providers (Guadamaz and Marsden 2015, pp. 11–12). Still, the example of the BitLicense regulation, introduced in New York, illustrates the challenge facing regulators. The BitLicense took two years to develop and, 'by the time it was enacted in 2015, the crypto world had moved on to smart contracts and ethereum' (Casey and Vigna 2018, pp. 53–54). Although the thinking behind the BitLicense was clear enough, it added costly burdens to acquiring and using digital currency (Casey and Vigna 2018, p. 195); numerous blockchain businesses simply ceased doing business in New York State (Roberts 2015; De Castillo 2015). Regional, and even national, solutions, then, can only ever be partially effective in regulating a globally distributed ledger:

> The decentralised, cross-boundary character of blockchain raises jurisdictional issues as it seems to diffuse institutional accountability and legal responsibility in an unprecedented manner, rendering the need for a more harmonised regulatory approach at the transnational level more pertinent compared with a local or regional one. (Boucher 2017, p. 23)

Globally, the attitude of politicians and policy-makers towards blockchain technology in general, and tokens in particular, is inconsistent at best. America's Securities and Exchange Commission, for instance, has warned investors against investing in token sales, while China has banned them altogether. This political uncertainty represents a significant barrier to adoption, while the inconsistency between countries hinders the development of standards. Artos CTO Andy Grant states in our interview that regulatory uncertainty is the biggest problem facing start-ups in the space:

> *O'Dair*: What one step could policy-makers take to promote the adoption of blockchain technology in the creative industries in what you would consider a positive manner?
>
> *Grant*: There's a while to go before the legal framework catches up with any new technology, and longer to go before any worldwide consensus is reached. At the moment, we're looking at a very fragmented legal landscape. We would welcome clarity in this area: if you don't know the rules it's hard to play the game! A worldwide consortium devoted to engaging with governments around the world, educating consumers, lobbying for adoption and demystifying the technology would be a good positive step to bringing about that clarity.

In our interview, Maecenas Fine Art CEO Marcelo Garcia Casil makes a similar point, although he seems to favour a more hands-off approach:

O'Dair: What one step could policy-makers take to promote the adoption of blockchain technology in the creative industries in what you would consider a positive manner?

Casil: There is currently very little in way of clear guidelines regarding the adoption of blockchain technology, the guidelines that do exist also vary significantly from one jurisdiction to the next. Imposed regulatory restrictions are paradoxical, as the basic premise of the blockchain was designed to be self-regulating and self-governing. So perhaps the best approach for regulators to promote the technology is to remain open-minded to this fast-growing technology and allow it to grow organically.

A final political challenge relates to data, and Casil also refers in our interview to the need for companies to act responsibly in this respect. The careful and responsible treatment of data is particularly important in the European context, given the recent introduction of General Data Protection Regulation (GDPR). Maintaining privacy on blockchains is already a concern for business (Deshpande et al. 2017, p. 7), and the GDPR has been described as in some respects incompatible with blockchain technology:

> Whereas the GDPR was fashioned for a world where data is centrally collected, stored, and processed, blockchains decentralise each of these processes… at least at first sight blockchains (especially those that are public and unpermissioned) and the GDPR are profoundly incompatible at a conceptual level as the data protection mechanisms developed for centralised data silos cannot be easily reconciled with a decentralised method of data storage and protection. (Finck 2018, p. 1)

Even before the GDPR came into force, Finck suggests, it was already partially outdated because of blockchain technology, as well as developments in big data and artificial intelligence. 'While law has always lagged behind technological change, this divide becomes more acute as the pace of innovation speeds up in the digital age' (Finck 2018, p. 28).

Economic

FilmChain co-founders Irina Albita and Maria Tanjala, along with community and content manager Jamie Sly, address the economic appeal of blockchain technology in our interview:

O'Dair: [How important is blockchain technology to your] operations (i.e. your human, intellectual, financial and physical resources, your day-to-day activities, and your partnerships)?

Albita et al.: In terms of operations, blockchain allows the automation of roles that would have previously taken individuals time to manually integrate and execute. This automation provided by blockchain allows the optimisation of business processes, enabling people to devote their time to the areas that matter, freeing up time from unnecessary workloads. We are consolidating partnerships with blockchain platforms and members of the ecosystem. We are in close communication with ConsenSys (ethereum) and we are part of EU Blockchain Observatory & Forum. It is key to keep updated on the latest developments, tools and regulations.

To the extent that blockchain technology is presented as radical/disruptive, we can expect it to be resisted by incumbents for the same reason that turkeys would not vote for Christmas. 'Incumbents that make money from the old system won't give up the golden goose quickly' (Casey and Vigna 2018, p. 235). This also represents a political barrier to adoption (see the 'Political' section above), since some of those that stand to gain from maintaining the status quo wield substantial lobbying power. That established organisations are slow to adopt the technology's more radical applications is also due to value networks; incumbents, as Christensen (2016) argues, are inherently inflexible and this makes them vulnerable to disruptive technologies. Christine Mohan of Civil argues in our interview for a first-mover advantage:

O'Dair: What is the biggest misconception about adopting blockchain technology within the creative industries?

Mohan: Some creative firms may feel that it's too early to investigate and adopt blockchain technology; that the technology is untested, not relevant; or that the consumer is not ready. Those who take a 'wait and see' approach will miss out on early industry developments and learnings. The time to experiment and build blockchain expertise is now.

As stated in Chapter 2, however, blockchains are not only a disruptive technology; there are also incorporative/sustaining applications. Incumbents are embracing blockchain technology as a means of improving efficiency. The incorporative dream, as Swartz (2017) argues, is not one of full decentralisation or disintermediation; instead, the incorporative vision concerns the use of private, permissioned blockchains to improve the process of mediation. Maecenas Fine Art CEO Marcelo Garcia Casil refers in his interview to resistance from incumbents:

O'Dair: What do you consider the main barriers to adoption, both within your company and beyond, and how might those barriers be overcome? Please consider political, economic, social, technological, legal and/or environmental factors.

Casil: The peer-to-peer nature of blockchain technology, where content creators can transact directly and immediately with content consumers—without middlemen—has implications for all creative industries: journalism and media, entertainment, film, music. Established players will inevitably create barriers to prevent these connections; creatives and consumers need to continue to push the boundaries and status quo.

Civil co-founder Christine Mohan makes a similar point in our interview:

O'Dair: What do you consider the risks—to your company and beyond—of adopting blockchain technology? Again, please consider political, economic, social, technological, legal and/or environmental factors.

Mohan: News consumers and media companies are core users and partners for Civil, yet few mainstream consumers understand blockchain or cryptocurrency. We need to offer exclusive, high-quality news experiences and drive usage from casual readers to community governance through token ownership. Beyond Civil, global media firms are currently investigating blockchain options and platforms, but may not be ready (strategically, psychologically or financially) to commit to such a nascent technology. Instead they may prefer to focus on emergent technologies (AR, VR, AI, machine learning) or continue to innovate within more familiar technologies (video, podcasts, mobile).

Of course, new entrants are proposing more radical applications—and, for Christensen (2016), they have an attacker's advantage with a disruptive technology such as blockchain. At the same time, new entrants do face significant barriers (Porter 1980). And even radical applications of blockchain technology may not be as radical as proponents expect. Any consideration of changing the shape of the firm (Coase 1937), something some expect DAOs to achieve, must pay heed to transaction cost economics (Williamson 1985). As McAfee and Brynjolfsson (2017) point out, the assumption underpinning the DAO was that every future decision could be adjudicated by a comprehensive contract—and yet, in practice, complete contracts simply do not exist. The world is an unpredictable place. Indeed, it can be argued that firms are necessary precisely because it is not possible for market participants to write complete contracts. Smart contracts, argue McAfee and Brynjolfsson (2017, p. 318), 'simply can't solve the problems of incomplete contracting and residual rights of control that a company solves by letting management make all the decisions not explicitly assigned to other parties'. Contracts are especially incomplete, Caves (2000, p. 14) suggests, in the creative industries, where 'nobody knows the value of a project until most or all resources have already been committed to it'.

An additional economic challenge is the volatility of cryptocurrencies, which threaten the stability of royalty payments. Bitcoin is of some use as a medium of exchange—it is possible to use it to buy and sell products—but is not a viable unit of account or store of value (Golumbia 2016, pp. 51–52). Tokens, too, tend to be volatile in terms of financial value (FCA 2017). This barrier could be overcome by using a cryptocurrency 'pegged' to a fiat currency or to gold, although there are some drawbacks to this approach. There is also, at present, a logistical economic challenge: blockchain start-ups struggle to open traditional bank accounts, although there is some evidence that the situation is begining to change.

Social

Distributed systems are, by their nature, prone to fragment—think of the splits within bitcoin and ethereum—and the proliferation of cryptocurrencies undermines network effects (Halaburda and Sarvary 2016, p. 159). Silver (2016) argues that multiple blockchains within a given industry would be a nightmare; Mougayar (2016, p. 57), by contrast, envisages a company participating in multiple blockchains and does not seem to regard such a scenario as problematic. Interoperability, and standards, are certainly critical (Tasca et al. 2017, p. 3) if we are to avoid simply building a new series of data silos using blockchain technology (Lundy-Bryan 2018). In the case of the internet, for instance, ICANN (Internet Corporation for Assigned Names and Numbers) has proved successful as a trusted central body. In a blockchain ecosystem predicated on resistance to centralisation, however, this is a significant challenge.

Despite the headlines and hype, adoption of bitcoin by people outside of the tech sector remains relatively low, partially because of its continuing association with criminality—for instance, the WannaCry ransomware attack of 2017 (Casey and Vigna 2018, p. 193). The same is true of blockchain technology more broadly. This is a point raised, in interviews conducted for this book, by Publica CEO Josef Marc and Civil co-founder Christine Mohan, as well as by Maecenas Fine Art CEO Marcelo Garcia Casil, who points out that many conflate bitcoin and blockchain. Artos CTO Andy Grant makes a similar point in our interview:

O'Dair: What is the biggest misconception about adopting blockchain technology within the creative industries?

Grant: As far as the layperson is concerned, there are a lot of misconceptions around blockchain—particularly around the volatility of cryptocurrencies, given that bitcoin is the most well-known use-case and is often conflated with the blockchain as a whole. There's a popular conception that blockchain is a buzzword and a bubble and people are just out to make a quick buck. Within the technical community itself, some blockchain advocates haven't fully considered the complexities of the problem they're trying to solve, which will ultimately affect the efficacy of solutions and their adoption.

Education, then, is key (Mougayar 2016, p. 80). Dan Fowler, Head of Strategy and Operations at JAAK, suggests in our interview that dispelling myths that surround blockhain technology is an important but time-consuming task for start-ups in the space:

O'Dair: What is the biggest misconception about adopting blockchain technology within the creative industries?

Fowler: A considerable amount of our time has been spent dispelling the 'blockchain myths' that have evolved over the past couple of years. Namely: (1) blockchains don't automatically solve data conflicts; (2) public blockchains don't require all data within them to be fully visible; and (3) perfect or minimum data is not a prerequisite—you cannot change history in a blockchain, but you can update information.

Adding to the social challenge is the fact that cryptocurrencies tend not to be very user-friendly (Tapscott and Tapscott 2018), although the situation is improving. The lack of blockchain developers (Mougayar 2016,

p. 68) is a further challenge. Who is going to build this brave new world? This is a point raised in interviews carried out for this book by respondents from JAAK and Filmchain, as well as by Christine Mohan of Civil:

O'Dair: What one step could policy-makers take to promote the adoption of blockchain technology in the creative industries in what you would consider a positive manner?

Mohan: Policy-makers could support the training of high school and community college students, across diverse backgrounds, to learn the programming languages needed for blockchain, smart contracts and cryptocurrency. Blockchain engineers are already in high demand; the pay is higher than many other software engineer roles, and a talented engineer can work from anywhere in the world. Today's journalism schools train students how to code; tomorrow's liberal arts programs need to train students in blockchain technologies.

Widespread adoption of cryptocurrencies is likely to involve support with private key management: some put the value of lost bitcoins at $950 million (Berke 2017). As Casey and Vigna (2018, p. 217) state, 'if you forget your password at work, you can ask the system administrator to create you a new one, but there's no-one managing the bitcoin blockchain who can do the same'. One solution could lie in multi-signature technology. Alternatively, adoption of blockchain technology in the creative economy might not require members of the public to own cryptocurrencies at all: payment could be made in fiat currencies, such as dollars and pounds, and the rest could happen beneath the bonnet (Mougayar 2016, p. 82). This is a point made in our interview by Blokur founder Phil Barry:

O'Dair: What is the biggest misconception about adopting blockchain technology within the creative industries?

Barry: Because blockchain is still a relatively new technology, very few user-facing products and services exist. As a result, people spend a lot of time talking about the underlying technology itself, rather than the thing that people and businesses will interact with. This sometimes has the effect of making it seem that blockchain technology will be difficult to adopt from a technology and systems perspective. In fact, it is perfectly possible that in many cases people will use an application that leverages blockchain technology without knowing that a blockchain is even being used.

Josef Marc states in his interview that Publica, likewise, are introducing a 'fiat layer', so that users can participate without owning cryptocurrency, and both Christine Mohan of Civil and Olivier Biggs of GUTS make similar points in interviews conducted for this book. For respondents from FilmChain, too, it is vital not to limit customer segments to those in possession of cryptocurrencies:

> *O'Dair*: [How important is blockchain technology to your] market (i.e. your customers, your relationships with those customers, and your channels for reaching those customers, before, during and after a sale)?
> *Albita et al.*: The channels of communication stay the same, film festival markets, industry publications, social media, word-of-mouth etc. We do not want to massively change behaviours for our customers, so we are somewhat hiding the complexity of the technology, while building user friendly and accessible interfaces. We want any producer, investor, financier, crew, actor, with any level of tech knowledge, to be able to use our platform.

Of course, even if users do not require cryptocurrency, industry buy-in is still necessary—and that too represents a social barrier to adoption, as Robert Norton, CEO of Verisart, states in our interview:

> *O'Dair*: What do you consider the main barriers to adoption, both within your company and beyond, and how might those barriers be overcome? Please consider political, economic, social, technological, legal and/or environmental factors.
> *Norton*: Our two biggest challenges are getting the art market to fully adopt distributed ledger technologies and promoting the widespread use of digital certification as part of the transaction of an artwork.

A final social barrier to adoption is the fact that, while smart contracts might be able to automatically pay creators their agreed splits every time a work is streamed, those splits still have to be agreed in the first place. However impressive the technology, it may be that artistic creation can never be quantified to the satisfaction of all parties: there will always be a number of truths. By making ownership shares more transparent, blockchain technology could even lead to a greater number of disputes. Given the complexity of social production, O'Dwyer (2017, p. 305) has gone as far as to question the very idea that that all forms of contribution to a cultural work can and should be remunerated.

Technological

While blockchain technology is attractive, it is also immature (Deshpande et al. 2017, p. 7); DApps, in particular, are nascent. The most obvious technological challenge is scalability (Hileman and Rauchs 2017, p. 68), a topic raised by interview respondents including Andy Grant of Artos and Bryce Bladon of CryptoKitties. Olivier Biggs, Communication and Community Manager at GUTS, also raises the subject in our interview:

> *O'Dair*: What do you consider the main barriers to adoption, both within your company and beyond, and how might those barriers be overcome? Please consider political, economic, social, technological, legal and/or environmental factors.
>
> *Biggs*: The first barrier is scalability. We plan on selling millions of tickets, for events that often release large batches of their tickets simultaneously. This means large amounts of traffic and transactions, that all need to go flawlessly. For this reason, we are constantly doing stress tests for our systems, that grow in scale and intensity each time, and include more and more edge cases, to achieve 100% success rate.

There is a lack of tools for developers (Mougayar 2016, p. 69) and ethereum is also buggy, which, given the context of unalterable smart contracts that manage money, is a major concern (Pearson 2018). For Casey and Vigna (2018, p. 147), 'open-to-all, permissionless blockchains such as bitcoin's and ethereum's simply aren't ready for the prime time of global trade'. Bitcoin cannot handle more than a few transactions a second, while ethereum, although faster, can fail to process transactions during busy periods (Casey and Vigna 2018. p. 131). Blockchain technology cannot—yet—meet demands from a technical perspective, for instance for high-performance, rapid transactions or the storage of large amounts of non-transactional data (Mulligan et al. 2018). That said, there are possible solutions are being explored, including the Lightning Network and ethereum's Plasma project, not to mention non-blockchain approaches to DLT such as the directed acyclic graph. Almost all the respondents interviewed for this book are using the ethereum blockchain, although Maecenas Fine Art are looking at running a private blockchain in addition and Verisart, unusually, use bitcoin. Yet CEO Josef Marc states in his interview that Publica will leave ethereum if necessary, and FilmChain also appear blockchain-agnostic.

Perhaps the two most challenging technological limitations facing blockchain relate to authenticity and provenance. As regards authenticity, there remains the problem, in using blockchains to register IP, that a creative work is not native to the blockchain: unlike a bitcoin, a painting, for instance, has a life beyond the ledger. Solving the 'garbage in/garbage out' issue is crucial, since no smart contract can make good data that is incorrect at the point of registration. Clearly untenable is a situation in which, either due to a genuine mistake, or to more malign motives, I am able to register myself as the composer of 'Hey Jude'. The risk, unless and until this problem is solved, is of 'creating an indisputable permanence to information that enshrines some abuse of a person's property rights' (Casey and Vigna 2018, p. 187), even if, as JAAK's Dan Fowler points out, the fact that you cannot 'change history' on a blockchain does not mean that information cannot be updated. Who, then, enters the information? What is their incentive? How is that information verified? How will the inevitable disputes be settled? There seem to be two possible answers. One is relatively centralised: a select group of people, for instance collection societies, take on the role of either entering, or validating, the data, and resolving disputes: a trusted third party, in other words, determines the accuracy of a given input (Hileman and Rauchs 2017, p. 18). The other solution is more decentralised: anyone can input data but good behaviour is incentivised through tokens and a reputation systems, through voting, or even through machine learning and probabilistic analysis of fraud (De Filippi et al. 2016, p. 6). There is also the important issue of legacy catalogue: the 'day zero' problem of how to address the millions of songs that already exist (Howard 2017, p. 180). One answer is to simply draw a line and agree to at least make the changes necessary for a better future rather than being forever restricted by an imperfect past. That legacy catalogue, pragmatists argue, could be dealt with further down the line.

The garbage in/garbage out problem, then, is essentially one of *authenticity*; it concerns registering a work on a blockchain in the first place. There is also a second problem, relating to *provenance*: the technology to copy files, Casey and Vigna (2018, p. 235) concede, will not go away, 'regardless of whether the first customer obtained the work from an artist who'd registered it in the blockchain'. How, then, do you stop someone 'breaking the chain' by taking a work outside the system? Registering an e-book on a blockchain would not prevent the circulation of photographs of its pages, just as registering a musical work would not prevent a user from making a copy, via an audio output, and then circulating it without permission. Registering works on a blockchain, then, is not enough; arguably, you would also require hardware that would only access content that is known to be owned or licensed by the owner of that hardware O'Dwyer (2017). Physical artefacts such as paintings are even more vulnerable to off-ledger transfers of ownership. While it may be that it is simply not possible to prevent users from 'breaking the chain', it may be sufficient to offer users a cost-effective and user-friendly legal alternative (this, after all, is how music streaming reduced the appeal of illegal downloads). Certainly, the buyer of a digital asset has an incentive to maintain the chain of provenance, as it will help maintain the value of the asset (De Filippi et al. 2016, p. 5). It would also be possible to address the problem through the issuance of tokens—either 'internal' tokens that denote IP rights, or 'external' tokens that reward creators even when their works are not protected by exclusive copyright (Ito and O'Dair, forthcoming). Finally, there may well be a role for content identification technology, similar to Shazam or Google Images search, to identify media based on how it sounds or looks (Howard 2017, pp. 198–9). In the future, machine learning is also likely to play a critical role.

Legal

Bitcoin operates in a 'legal grey area' (Grindberg 2011, p. 207), largely because, as Evans (2015, p. 106) points out, we can understand it in different ways: as commodity, base money, currency, database, transaction history and so on. Bitcoin can resemble a money transmittal system, or a commodity, or a share of stock; some consider it a currency, others do not. Those tasked with regulating bitcoin, Evans suggests, are akin to blind monks confronting an elephant. The regulator holding a tusk is not going to understand it in the same way as the regulator touching the trunk. This is also true of other cryptocurrencies.

The introduction of smart contracts has been accompanied by the widespread proclamation that 'code is law'. This claim derives from Lessig (2006) but it 'has become normative ideal rather than a critical observation' (Myers 2017, p. 245); Lessig states quite clearly that there are many important differences between code and law, even if code and law also, at least to a certain extent, do the same job. Yet the emergence of blockchain technology has only emphasised 'a tension between the jurisdictional claims of code-is-law and the law of the land' (Myers 2017, p. 246). Indeed:

> Part of the attraction of distributed ledger systems, such as blockchain, lies in transcending law and regulation. From a technological perspective, DLT is generally seen as offering unbreakable security, immutability and unparalleled transparency, so law and regulation are seen as unnecessary. Yet while the law may be dull and the technology exciting, the impact of law cannot simply be wished away. (Zetzsche et al. 2017, p. 1)

In particular, there is a lack of clarity regarding smart contracts (Deshpande et al. 2017, p. 7), and tokens (Conley 2017). As Maecenas CEO Marcelo Garcia Casil states in our interview, the company has had to tread carefully in working out how to tokenise artworks:

> *O'Dair*: What do you consider the main barriers to adoption, both within your company and beyond, and how might those barriers be overcome? Please consider political, economic, social, technological, legal and/or environmental factors.
>
> *Casil*: This is a completely new model that has never been done before in the art market, and one of the biggest challenges we had was to ensure that from legal and compliance standpoint we had a firm and strong infrastructure for the asset-backed securities. However, we are consistently receiving encouraging feedback and validation from experts in the industry who are just as excited as we are about the new direction and opportunities that Maecenas can provide to revolutionise the art investment market and the industry as a whole.

Token sales present a particular challenge, since they offer no investor protection and may be fraudulent (FCA 2017). There is also the vexed question of precisely which cryptographic assets do, and do not, qualify as securities. There are a whole range of possible regulatory responses (Kaal 2018) and different countries are taking different approaches, for instance in terms of the regulation of cryptocurrency exchanges. In general, in fact, the attitudes of governments towards blockchain technology is varied (Kaal 2018, p. 22). 'As long as the position of regulators is not clarified,' Mougayar (2016, p. 77) suggests, 'confusion and uncertainty will continue to exist for everyone involved in the blockchain space'. In our interview, Publica CEO Josef Marc raises the fact that potential users in India are unable to participate because they are prohibited from holding cryptocurrencies.

In the UK context, finally, Brexit is a particular legal (as well as political) concern, as Blokur's Phil Barry notes in our interview:

O'Dair: What one step could policy-makers take to promote the adoption of blockchain technology in the creative industries in what you would consider a positive manner?

Barry: The single most helpful thing UK policy-makers could do would be to guarantee the UK's future membership of the European single market and European copyright framework.

Environmental

Finally, some businesses are put off by the energy-intensive nature of blockchain technology:

> The distributed nature of DLT/blockchain (in which changes are made to multiple ledgers simultaneously) means that certain ledger designs may be significantly more energy intensive than centralised alternatives. This is likely to be a more significant problem for permissionless ledgers than for permissioned ones, in which scaling can be planned and managed. With large numbers of stakeholders and technologies (with different approaches to DLT/blockchain implementation), the energy costs of running such a system and ensuring that effective cost-estimation mechanisms are in place (particularly on the server side to manage demand) may pose a significant challenge. (Deshpande et al. 2017, p. 16)

Miners (for proof-of-work blockchains) tend to gravitate to locations in which energy is cheap, leaving them vulnerable to changes in energy prices. This is an issue on the minds of start-ups and a potential barrier to adoption: it is mentioned in interviews conducted for this book by Publica's Josef Marc, Artos CTO Andy Grant and Bryce Bladon of CryptoKitties. I examine these environmental risks in more detail in Chapter 5.

Conclusion

Blockchain technology is potentially transformative, but it is not going to achieve immediate mainstream adoption. Innovation, as so often, is beginning in the margins. And, as Perez (2002) argues, the wealth-creating potential of technological revolutions is not immediately realised. Blockchains, like other new and disruptive technologies, face significant political, economic, social, technological, legal and environmental barriers to adoption. There is a clear role here for policy-makers, as respondents from FilmChain suggest in our interview:

O'Dair: What one step could policy-makers take to promote the adoption of blockchain technology in the creative industries in what you would consider a positive manner?

Albita et al.: Governments should actively try to promote Blockchain technology by:

- Providing more R&D funding for tech companies to explore the benefits.
- Drafting a clear regulatory framework to govern the launch and growth of blockchain-driven initiatives.
- Supporting more education around the space by commissioning industry papers, organising trade working groups and collaborating with universities.

I return to these suggestions in Chapter 6. First, in Chapter 5, I examine risks to blockchain adoption, again using the PESTLE framework.

References

Bakhshi, H., and E. Lomas. 2017. Defining R&D for the Creative Industries. *Nesta*. https://ahrc.ukri.org/documents/project-reports-and-reviews/policy-briefing-digital-r-d/. Accessed 14 May 2018.

Berke, A. 2017. How Safe Are Blockchains? It Depends. *Harvard Business Review*. https://hbr.org/2017/03/how-safe-are-blockchains-it-depends. Accessed 4 May 2018.

Boucher, P. 2017. How Blockchain Technology Could Change Our Lives. European Parliamentary Research Service.

Casey, M., and P. Vigna. 2018. *The Truth Machine: The Blockchain and the Future of Everything*. London: Harper Collins.

Caves, R. 2000. *Creative Industries: Contracts Between Art and Commerce*. Cambridge, MA: Harvard University Press.

Christensen, C. 2016. *The Innovator's Dilemma: When New Technologies Cause Great Firms to Fail*. Boston: Harvard Business Review Press.

Coase, R. 1937. The Nature of the Firm. *Economica* 4 (16): 386–405.

Conley, J. 2017. Blockchain and the Economics of Crypto-Tokens and Initial Coin Offerings. Working Paper Series, Vanderbilt University, Department of Economics. http://www.accessecon.com/Pubs/VUECON/VUECON-17-00008.pdf. Accessed 10 November 2017.

De Castillo, M. 2015. The 'Great Bitcoin Exodus' Has Totally Changed New York's Bitcoin Ecosystem. *New York Business Journal*. https://www.bizjournals.com/newyork/news/2015/08/12/the-great-bitcoin-exodus-has-totally-changed-new.html. Accessed 2 March 2018.

De Filippi, P., G. McMullen, T. McConaghy, C. Choi, S. de la Rouviere, J. Benet, and D. Stern. 2016. How Blockchains Can Support, Complement, or Supplement Intellectual Property: Working Draft, Version 1.0, COALA. http://docplayer.net/56177308-How-blockchains-can-support-complement-or-supplement-intellectual-property.html. Accessed 4 May 2018.

Deshpande, A., K. Stewart, L. Lepetit, and S. Gunashekar. 2017. *Distributed Ledger Technologies/Blockchain: Challenges, Opportunities, and the Prospects for Standards*. London: BSI/ Rand Europe.

Evans, C. 2015. The Blind Economists and the Elephant: Bitcoin and Monetary Separation. *Southwestern Journal of Economics* 10 (1): 106–122.

FCA. 2017. Initial Coin Offerings. https://www.fca.org.uk/news/statements/initial-coin-offerings. Accessed 2 March 2018.

Finck, M. 2018. Blockchains and Data Protection in the European Union. Max Plank Institute for Innovation and Competition. Research Paper No. 18-01.

Golumbia, D. 2016. *The Politics of Bitcoin: Software as Right-Wing Extremism*. Minneapolis: University of Minnesota Press.
Grindberg, R. 2011. Bitcoin: An Innovative Alternative Digital Currency. *Hastings Science & Technology Law Journal* 4: 160–211.
Guadamaz, A., and C. Marsden. 2015. Blockchains and Bitcoin: Regulatory Responses. *First Monday* 20 (12): 1–37.
Halaburda, H., and M. Sarvary. 2016. *Beyond Bitcoin: The Economics of Digital Currencies*. Basingstoke: Palgrave Macmillan.
Hesmondhalgh, D. 2007. *The Cultural Industries*, 2nd ed. London: Sage.
Hileman, G., and M. Rauchs. 2017. Global Blockchain Benchmarking Study. https://papers.ssrn.com/sol3/papers.cfm?abstract_id=3040224. Accessed 24 March 2018.
Howard, G. 2017. *Everything in Its Right Place: How Blockchain Technology Will Lead to a More Transparent Music Industry*. Beverly Farms, MA: 9GiantSteps.
Ito, K., and M. O'Dair. Forthcoming. A Critical Examination of the Application of Blockchain Technology for Intellectual Property Management. In *Implications of the Blockchain*, ed. H. Treiblmaier. Basingstoke: Palgrave Macmillan.
Kaal, W. 2018. Initial Coin Offerings: The Top 25 Jurisdictions and Their Comparative Regulatory Responses. Research Paper No. 18-07, University of St. Thomas Legal Studies. https://papers.ssrn.com/sol3/papers.cfm?abstract_id=3117224. Accessed 4 May 2018.
Kaplanov, N. 2012. Nerdy Money: Bitcoin, the Private Digital Currency, and the Case Against Its Regulation. *Loyola Consumer Law Review* 25 (1): 111–171.
Kiviat, T. 2015. Beyond Bitcoin: Issues in Regulating Blockchain Transactions. *Duke Law Journal* 65: 569–608.
Lehdonvirta, V., and R. Ali. 2016. Governance and Regulation. Distributed Ledger Technology: Beyond Blockchain. https://www.gov.uk/government/uploads/system/uploads/attachment_data/file/492972/gs-16-1-distributed-ledger-technology.pdf. Accessed 2 March 2018.
Lessig, L. 2006. *Code Version 2.0*. New York: Basic Books.
Lundy-Bryan, L. 2018. Building the Internet of Blockchains. https://outlierventures.io/research/convergence-ecosystem-forget-blockchain-applications-without-this-one-special-trick/. Accessed 22 June 2018.
McAfee, A., and E. Brynjolfsson. 2017. *Machine Platform Crowd: Harnessing Our Digital Future*. New York and London: Norton.
Mougayar, W. 2016. *The Business Blockchain: Promise, Practice and Application of the Next Internet Technology*. Hoboken: Wiley.

Mulligan, C.J., Z. Scott, S. Warren, and J.P. Rangaswami. 2018. *Blockchain Beyond the Hype*. World Economic Forum. http://www3.weforum.org/docs/48423_Whether_Blockchain_WP.pdf. Accessed 2 May 2018.

Myers, R. 2017. Blockchain Poetics. In *Artists Re: Thinking the Blockchain*, ed. R. Catlow, M. Garrett, N. Jones, and S. Skinner. Liverpool: Liverpool University Press.

Narayanan, A., J. Bonneau, E. Felten, A. Miller, and S. Goldfeder. 2016. *Bitcoin and Cryptocurrency Technologies: A Comprehensive Introduction*. Princeton and Oxford: Princeton University Press.

O'Dwyer, R. 2017. Does Digital Culture Want to Be Free? How Blockchains Are Transforming the Economy of Cultural Goods. In *Artists Re:Thinking the Blockchain*, ed. R. Catlow, M. Garrett, N. Jones, and S. Skinner. Liverpool: Liverpool University Press.

Pearson, J. 2018. Millions of Dollars in Ethereum Are Vulnerable to Hackers Right Now. *Motherboard*. https://motherboard.vice.com/en_us/article/8xddka/millions-of-dollars-in-ethereum-are-vulnerable-to-hackers-right-now-smart-contract-bugs. Accessed 8 May 2018.

Perez, C. 2002. *Technological Revolutions and Financial Capital: The Dynamics of Bubbles and Golden Ages*. Cheltenham: Edward Elgar.

Porter, M. 1980. *Competitive Strategy: Techniques for Analysing Industries and Competitors*. London: Free Press.

PWC. 2017. Introduction to Token Sales (ICO) Best Practices. https://www.pwccn.com/en/financial-services/publications/introduction-to-token-sales-ico-best-practices.pdf. Accessed 2 March 2018.

Roberts, D. 2015. Behind the 'Exodus' of Bitcoin Startups from New York. *Fortune*. http://fortune.com/2015/08/14/bitcoin-startups-leave-new-york-bitlicense/. Accessed 2 March 2018.

Silver, J. 2016. Blockchain or the Chaingang? Challenges, Opportunities and Hype: The Music Industry and Blockchain Technologies. CREATe Working Paper. www.create.ac.uk/publications/blockchain-or-the-chaingang-challenges-opportunities-and-hype-the-music-industry-and-blockchain-technologies/. Accessed 14 May 2018.

Swartz, L. 2017. Blockchain Dreams: Imagining Techno-Economic Alternatives After Bitcoin. In *Another Economy Is Possible: Culture and Economy in a Time of Crisis*, ed. M. Castells. Cambridge: Polity.

Tapscott, D., and A. Tapscott. 2018. *Blockchain Revolution: How the Technology Behind Bitcoin and Other Cryptocurrencies Is Changing the World*, Updated ed. New York:Penguin Random House.

Tasca, P., T. Thayabaran, and C. Tessone. 2017. Ontology of Blockchain Technologies: Principles of Identification and Classification. https://papers.ssrn.com/sol3/papers.cfm?abstract_id=2977811. Accessed 25 August 2017.

Williamson, O.E. 1985. *The Economic Institutions of Capitalism*. New York: Free Press.

Wright, A., and P. De Filippi. 2015. Decentralised Blockchain Technology and the Rise of Lex Cryptographia. https://papers.ssrn.com/sol3/papers.cfm?abstract_id=2580664. Accessed 2 March 2028.

Zetzsche, D., R. Buckley, and D. Arner. 2017. The Distributed Liability of Distributed Ledgers: Legal Risks of Blockchain. Law Working Paper Series number 2017-007. University of New South Wales Law Research Series.

CHAPTER 5

Risks of Adoption

Abstract Disruptive technologies create losers as well as winners. We cannot anticipate all possible consequences, but we should at least try to consider the risks, as well as the benefits, to the creative economy (and beyond) in adopting blockchain technology. In *political* terms, both a complete lack of appropriate regulation, on the one hand, and over-regulation, on the other, represent risks. In *economic* terms, the removal of trusted third parties may not be as desirable as tech-utopians assume. In terms of *social* risks, we should remember that decentralised technologies do not necessarily decentralise power; the asymmetries of wealth and power evident in our own society may simply be replicated, or even accentuated, on a blockhain. As regards *technological* risks, blockchains could facilitate the illegal storage of digital works in a way that, because it is distributed rather than centralised, makes the content very difficult to remove. This is also a *legal* risk, since 'notice and takedown' procedures would be ineffective in such a scenario. Arguably, there is a fundamental antipathy between blockchain technology and the very notion of copyright. Finally, there are significant *environmental* risks presented by the energy-intensive nature of mining.

Keywords Blockchain regulation · Collection societies · Power asymmetries · Blockchain piracy · Blockchain and copyright · Blockchain and the environment

M. O'Dair, *Distributed Creativity*,
https://doi.org/10.1007/978-3-030-00190-2_5

For all the potential, blockchain, like all new technologies, also presents risks. We would do well to remember Kranzberg's first law:

> Technology is neither good nor bad; nor is it neutral. By that I mean that technology's interaction with the social ecology is such that technical developments frequently have environmental, social and human consequences that go far beyond the immediate purposes of the technical devices and practices themselves, and the same technology can have quite different results when introduced into different contexts or under different circumstances. (Kranzberg 1995, p. 5)

Having examined 'the good' in Chapter 3, I turn in this chapter to 'the bad'. Assuming the various barriers can be overcome, what might be the risks for the creative economy in adopting blockchain technology? What might be the unintended consequences? I examine these risks below, again using the PESTLE framework.

Political

Tokens, in particular, represent a Wild West that some would like to see at least partially tamed. Yet both a complete lack of appropriate regulation, on the one hand, and over-regulation, on the other, represent risks to the blockchain ecosystem. Bitcoin's original users tend to favour the former, minimal regulation approach. A core principle of cyberlibertarianism, after all, is that governments should not regulate the internet. Excessive regulation is also a concern for businesses utilising blockchain technology: so-called enterprise applications. In interviews conducted for this book, respondents from FilmChain referred to excessive legal and regulatory restrictions as a danger, while Robert Norton of Verisart cited regulatory uncertainty as a risk facing his company. Over-regulation, it is widely acknowledged, can stifle innovation. As Casey and Vigna (2018, p. 54) state, 'one risk is that regulators, confused by all these outside-the-box concepts, will overreact to some bad news' by introducing 'a new set of draconian measures [that] would such the life out of innovation in this space or drive it offshore or underground'.

As I suggested in Chapter 4, however, many businesses using blockchain, as well as those cryptocurrency users who may have come to the space more recently than the original bitcoin cypherpunks, would welcome greater regulatory clarity, if not actually additional regulation.

Events such as the DAO disaster of 2016, or the hacking of the Mt. Gox bitcoin exchange back in 2014, are accepted by some cryptocurrency users as simply par for the course. Others, however, might find themselves missing those trusted third parties when an exchange is hacked or they lose their private keys. 'Risk does not vanish if financial services are provided via distributed ledgers', as Zetzsche et al. (2017, p. 8) point out; instead, it is simply distributed between participants. That blockchains are ostensibly decentralised and uncontrollable might be part of the appeal, suggest McAfee and Brynjolfsson (2017, p. 317), but what recourse is available if they begin to operate in a way users do not like?

Certainly, regulators need to proceed with caution. Faced with over-regulation, the crypto community will find workarounds; this, after all, is an inherently distributed technology associated with both heavy-duty cryptography and the dark net. In fact, governments should be working to attract blockchain companies, which naturally migrate to blockchain-friendly countries. The United Kingdom was at one point relatively advanced in blockchain terms, a position reflected by the publication of the Walport report in 2016 (even if the report neglected creative economy applications of the technology). However, the UK now risks falling behind the likes of Singapore and Dubai (Holmes 2017, p. 1). Switzerland, especially the so-called 'crypto valley' in and around Zug, is another favoured location (PWC 2017). Other countries cited as favourable for blockchain businesses include the Cayman Islands (Scherbin 2018), Liechtenstein and Mauritius (Thompson (2017), Malta (Fintech Times 2018), and Gibraltar (Alois 2018). While those interviewed for this book are not necessarily representative of blockchain businesses around the world, it is noteworthy that, even though my selection is skewed towards the UK by my own location in that country, several respondents are based overseas. Verisart is based in the UK and the US; Civil is based in the US but its team includes members in Poland; CryptoKitties is based in Canada; GUTS is based in the Netherlands; Publica is based in Gibraltar, although has an office in Latvia; and Maecenas, finally, has offices in Singapore, Switzerland and Argentina as well as the UK.

In fact, according to a recent piece by Tapscott and Tapscott (2018), London is only the eighth most likely location to become the 'Silicon Valley of blockchain'—after New York City, Singapore, Silicon Valley, Zurich/Zug, the Toronto-Waterloo Corridor, Beijing and Seoul. (Even though blockchain is an inherently distributed technology, it is reasonable to predict that it will still have one or more geographical centres, just as, for web 2.0, all the Slack channels in the world cannot overcome the physical pull of Silicon Valley.) The Tapscott and Tapscott article is light-hearted, presented as a 'blockchain World Cup' rather than rigorous research, but the underlying points are worthy of attention. Tapscott and Tapscott reach their conclusion after examining a number of factors, including government support and funding, size of regional market, ecosystem (of innovators, researchers, investors, developers and users), banking landscape, thought leadership (especially through research), private funding (especially venture capital), communities of talent (immigration and education), corporate leadership and regulatory clarity (Blockchain Research Institute 2018). In general, Tapscott and Tapscott note, the UK has a reasonable level of start-up activity and is an international centre of banking and commerce. They also note the success of fintech 'sandboxes', and the regulatory sandbox launched by the Financial Conduct Authority (FCA) was a noteworthy attempt to allow firms 'to test innovative products, services and business models in a live market environment' (FCA 2017). The sandbox was deemed a success, and a global sandbox is now being considered. As well as banks, London has what Tapscott and Tapscott call 'communities of talent', due to its immigration policies and strong university sector, and also does well in terms of thought leadership, due to its strengths in research. Yet the UK falls behind in terms of government support and funding, size of regional market, regularity clarity and openness, ecosystem, private funding and corporate leadership, while the imminence of Brexit raises questions relating to immigration. This should be a major concern for policy-makers aiming to make Britain the best place in the world to base both forward-looking start-ups and innovative larger organisations.

Economic

Some applications of blockchain technology, I have suggested, are incorporative/sustaining, while others are radical/disruptive. Those more radical start-ups using the technology to enable artists to control their own parameters for selling and licensing creative works represent an economic risk as well as exciting opportunities. This is because, economically as well as politically, the removal of trusted third parties may not be as desirable as advocates assume. As I outlined in Chapter 3, Howard (2017) suggests that blockchain technology could be used to allow creators to control their intellectual property themselves, rather than working with intermediaries such as collection societies. Howard is one of the few commentators in this space with a genuine understanding of the music industry, as well as of blockchain technology, yet his view on the desirability of removing collection societies is contentious. It can be argued that allowing creators, rather than intermediaries, to control licensing would simply make licensing even more complex. And while it might be possible for artists to withdraw from collection societies and directly license tracks via smart contracts, this would not be desirable for the bulk of artists since it would reduce the ability of collection societies to issue blanket licenses. Such a scenario would benefit a few star artists, no doubt, but it would disadvantage the majority. This is because, for less established artists, collection societies are akin to trade unions: a means of collective bargaining (Schroff and Street 2017). In the traditional collective management organisation model, in other words, more commercially successful creators cross-subsidise those who are less successful. Removing collection societies, then, could be seen as aligned with what some regard as an inherent quality of blockchain technology: a winner-takes-all outlook. For Golumbia (2016, p. 4), bitcoin's values 'incorporate critical parts of a right-wing worldview even as they manifest a surface rhetorical commitment to values that do not immediately appear to come from the right'. Golumbia argues that this extreme right-wing perspective underpins not only bitcoin but all blockchain applications. That said, there are also left-leaning blockchain projects, such as Resonate, a music-streaming co-operative, and scholars such as O'Dwyer (2017), Dodd (2017), and Huckle and White (2016) argue that blockchains can in fact be favoured by both libertarians, on the one hand, and socialists (and indeed anarchists) on the other.

Another economic risk is the fact that, as Blokur's Phil Barry mentioned in our interview, many start-ups are now heavily dependent on ethereum. This was also mentioned by respondents from FilmChain:

O'Dair: What do you consider the risks – to your company and beyond – of adopting blockchain technology? Again, please consider political, economic, social, technological, legal and/or environmental factors.

Albita et al.: Some of the main risks that come with the adoption of blockchain technology for our company and others are the potential regulatory and legal restrictions that could be put in place. There are also issues surrounding settlements and if the blockchain ledger is evidence of ownership from a legal and regulatory perspective. Technologically, while we are developing as protocol-agnostic as possible, we do have a massive buy-in into the ethereum platform – the blockchain protocol with the largest support communities. The way this protocol will develop and the strength of its governance systems are very important for us.

Social

Blockchain technology could bring many benefits, Casey and Vigna (2018) state, yet the net effect will not necessarily be positive:

> We've seen how the internet was co-opted by corporations and how that centralisation was caused problems – from creating big siloes of personal data for shady hackers to steal to incentivising disinformation campaigns that distort our democracy. So, it's crucial that we not let the people with the greatest capacity to influence this technology shape it to suit only their narrow interests... By definition, getting blockchain technology right requires input from all sectors of society. (Casey and Vigna 2018, pp. 14–15)

As it stands, all sectors of society do *not* have equal input into this technology. It is reported, for instance, that only 5–7% of cryptocurrency users are women (Lam 2017). Although I include women among my interview respondents, a 'blockchain bro' culture is dominant. Women and people of colour are significantly underrepresented in the tech sector more broadly (Tapscott and Tapscott 2017, p. 25). Given that technology reflects the value of those who create it (Zeilinger 2016, p. 22), the lack of diversity among blockchain developers, and even users of cryptocurrency, represents a significant social risk. Far from being decentralised by blockchain technology, it can be argued that society is in danger of being restructured by a handful of technocrats (Catlow 2017, p. 27).

Decentralised technology, as Catlow (2017) states, does not necessarily result in decentralised power. Far from being decentralised and democratic, Dodd (2017) suggests, bitcoin is characterised by asymmetries of wealth and power that are not too distant from those evident in the mainstream financial system. According to one media report (Murphy 2018), a group of just 1600 'whales' control one-third of the bitcoin market; according to another report, 95% of bitcoins are held by just 4% of owners (Bowles 2018). The power of miners, too, is consolidating (Tasca 2015; Tasca et al. 2017; McAfee and Brynjolfsson 2017; Narayanan et al. 2016). It can be argued that bitcoin has become increasingly centralised in recent years, as professional mining pools have been established, typically in locations with low electricity costs:

> Taken together, this brutal economic calculus, and the scale of investment that's now required to set up a mining operation that has even the slightest chance of turning a profit, bring strong centripetal forces to bear on the shape of the network. (Greenfield 2017, p. 138)

Bitcoin, then, is arguably 'a tool for existing power to concentrate itself, rather than a challenge to the existing order' (Golumbia 2016, p. 63). Ethereum, which is stewarded by a non-profit foundation, is even more centralised (Narayanan et al. 2016, p. 270). There is also no reason to assume that the interests of those utilising blockchain technology will be aligned with the interests of creators. Smart contracts, for instance, will not necessarily be used to empower artists or users: they could, for instance, be used as a new form of digital rights management, heavily restricting the use of content (De Filippi et al. 2016, p. 3). Arguably, it is naive to believe that commercial digital art markets based on blockchain technologies will empower artists at all:

> Once decentralised technologies are folded into proprietary, commercial products and services, models of centralised finance will be far from being disrupted but rather reinforced. The fact that such technologies are cryptographically secure might simply mean that the centralisation efforts they ultimately represent will be difficult, if not impossible, to counteract. (Zeilinger 2016, p. 37)

Technological

De Filippi and Wright (2018) argue that blockchains pose technological risks, since no single party has the power to remove references to content that a blockchain might store:

> As opposed to existing file sharing networks that rely on centralised intermediaries, these services operate autonomously using a blockchain and a software protocol to coordinate the exchange and dissemination of content. Once references to files are stored on a blockchain, they become difficult to remove, without invalidating the relevant blockchain as a whole. These platforms are thus constructed in a way that makes it possible for people to share content in ways that are difficult to halt. (De Filippi and Wright 2018, p. 120)

There are also technological risks posed by developments in quantum computing, which could challenge the cryptographic security upon which blockchain technology rests (Casey and Vigna 2018, p. 32n), although there has been some progress in this field of late.

Finally, the adoption of blockchain technology, like any nascent technology, can pose risks for individual businesses: as I argue in Chapter 6, disruptive technologies typically underperform in the short-term, at least by traditional measures. Blokur founder Phil Barry acknowledges this fact in our interview, but also downplays its longer-term significance:

> *O'Dair*: What do you consider the risks – to your company and beyond – of adopting blockchain technology? Again, please consider political, economic, social, technological, legal and/or environmental factors.
>
> *Barry*: Today's blockchains have well-reported limitations of scale and cost-efficiency that will need to be overcome. Therefore, there is some risk in the need to rely on future upgrades and improvements. But history suggests that, while it's difficult to predict which implementation is going to be the most successful, the market will drive the necessary innovation to bring the technology to maturity. In the meantime, it's necessary to build applications in a modular way to reduce dependency on any one blockchain technology.

Legal

Blockchain technology could lead 'to a reduced role for one of the most important regulatory actors in our society: the middleman' (Wright and De Filippi 2015, p. 1). For some, of course, this is precisely the appeal. Yet there are significant legal risks: 'by operating outside of a regulatory framework, blockchain-based organisations that are not incorporated or legally recognised may be at risk of investment fraud and malicious hacks, and their members could be exposed to liabilities as partners' (Boucher 2017, p. 21). As mentioned in our interview by Bryce Bladon, founding member of the CryptoKitties team, there are bad actors in this space, as in any other. These bad actors could, for instance, make use of the transnational, encrypted, decentralised and pseudonymous nature of blockchain technology to conduct illicit transactions, posing a major challenge for law enforcement agencies (Wight and De Filippi 2015).

This is already a challenge—and over time, as Wright and De Filippi point out, smart contracts and overlay networks are only likely to increase in sophistication:

> New blockchain-based services governed by lex cryptographia could provide large repositories of music, films, images, and books hosted on millions of computers across the globe in an easily accessible and searchable format. These systems could be designed to ignore copyright laws and would continue to operate so long as users provide the underlying smart contracts with sufficient fees to store data and execute software logic. In the end, code—not laws—could increasingly shape how information is disseminated worldwide. (De Filippi and Wright 2018, pp. 120–121)

For De Filippi and Wright (2018, p. 117), there is a fundamental antipathy between blockchain technology and copyright, since blockchains—at least in their original, cypherpunk incarnation—'aim to break down the "barbed wire" of copyright law, while simultaneously supporting platforms that could help spread indecent, obscene or inflammatory information.' Blockchain-based systems, Wright and De Filippi continue, are incompatible with notice and takedown procedures of the Digital Millennium Copyright Act and Electronic Commerce Directive, which requires online intermediaries to remove or disable access to infringing material once they have received notice from a copyright owner. This 'notice and takedown' process is already a game of whack-a-mole. Introducing blockchain technology, particularly in combination with decentralised file-sharing applications and overlay networks, could make them even less effective: 'If blockchain-based systems and applications operate independently of centralised operators, no single party will have the capacity to respond to a takedown notification by removing the allegedly infringing content' (De Filippi and Wright 2018, p. 124).

In intellectual property terms, the risk of new, decentralised forms of piracy is significant. De Filippi et al. (2016, p. 3) also raise the opposite concern: that blockchain technology will be used by rights holders to replicate the worst aspects of digital rights management. What if a smart contract is used, for instance, to charge every time an e-book reader turns a page or a gamer clicks 'save'? As Lessig argued back in 2006 (p. 175), the danger of code displacing law as the primary defence of IP in cyberspace is not that copyright is threatened—it is that 'copyright is more effectively protected than at any time since Gutenberg.' The question we should ask, Lessig argues, is not: how can law aid in that protection? It is, instead, is the protection too great?

Environmental

According to O'Dwyer and Malone (2014), the energy being used for bitcoin mining, even a few years ago, was already comparable to that consumed by Ireland. More recently, bitcoin's energy consumption has been compared to that of Austria (De Vries 2018) and Chile (Digiconomist 2018). Some have suggested that energy concerns are overplayed, but proof-of-work consensus mechanisms are certainly energy-intensive, and this is a major ecological concern (Tasca et al. 2017; Greenfield 2017; Nadal and Andaluz 2017). Josef Marc, Andy Grant and Bryce Bladon made reference to this environmental risk in our interviews. For Grant, however, it is likely to be a relatively short-term issue, solved by a shift from proof-of-work to proof-of-stake ('skin in the game') consensus mechanisms. Encouraging 'greener' approaches should certainly be a priority for policy-makers. Bitcoin may have been portrayed in a popular Reddit meme as 'magic internet money' but it is, in fact, dependent upon a very physical infrastructure. The internet 2.0 sits on top of the internet 1.0—and that, as Blum (2013) reminds us, runs upon a network of 'tubes.' While media infrastructures might appear ethereal, they are in fact 'grounded in bunker-like facilities heavily secured on earth,' and depend on 'lands, raw materials, and energy' (Parks and Starosielski 2015: 4–5). Proof-of-work consensus mechanisms are particularly problematic: bitcoin mining is dependent upon 'mega' data centres (Rossiter 2016: 165). The bitcoin network has been estimated to currently consume at least 2.55 gigawatts of electricity, a figure, we are told, that could rise to 7.67 gigawatts in the not-too-distant future (De Vries 2018); for the sake of comparison, Ireland uses 3.1 gigawatts, Austria 8.2. The average electricity consumed per transaction could exceed 900 kWh per transaction by the end of 2018 (De Vries 2018). In other words, 'bitcoin has a big problem, and it is growing fast' (De Vries 2018: 805). In the Anthropocene era (Bonneuil and Fressoz 2013), we should take the environmental risk very seriously indeed.

Conclusion

The interview data I collected from respondents tended to concern opportunities and barriers rather than risks. In general, blokchain advocates tend towards the tech-utopian. We know from history, however, that disruptive technologies create winners and losers. As Kranzberg

(1995) argued in his 'first law', we need to consider the environmental, social and human consequences of adopting any technology. Blockchain is no different. The need to interrogate the ethics of blockchain technology has increasingly been highlighted by academics, for instance Elsden et al. (2018):

> Many of the potential ethical challenges are familiar. What biases will be encoded into blockchain code? Who are blockchain applications for? Who do they empower and who is left at the margins?... while for example bitcoin and ethereum's ledgers are public and immutable, are these truly auditable and scrutable by regulators or end-users? When is such transparency idealistic or inadequate? What power do the core developers and foundations developing these protocols hold? (Elsden et al. 2018, p. 10)

References

Alois, J.D. 2018. Gibraltar's Blockchain Regulatory Framework Is Now in Effect. *Crowdfund Insider*. https://www.crowdfundinsider.com/2018/01/126582-gibraltars-blockchain-regulatory-framework-now-effect/. Accessed 27 June 2018.

Blockchain Research Institute. 2018. The Blockchain World Cup. https://www.blockchainresearchinstitute.org/blockchain-world-cup/. Accessed 26 June 2018.

Blum, A. 2013. *Tubes: Behind the Scenes at the Internet*. London: Penguin.

Bonneuil, C., and J.-B. Fressoz. 2013. *The Shock of the Anthropocene: The Earth, History and Us*. London: Verso.

Boucher, P. 2017. *How Blockchain Technology Could Change Our Lives*. European Parliamentary Research Service.

Bowles, N. 2018. Everyone Is Getting Hilariously Rich and You're Not. *New York Times*. https://www.nytimes.com/2018/01/13/style/bitcoin-millionaires.html. Accessed 4 May 2018.

Casey, M., and P. Vigna. 2018. *The Truth Machine: The Blockchain and the Future of Everything*. London: Harper Collins.

Catlow, R. 2017. Artists Re:Thinking the Blockchain Introduction. In *Artists Re:Thinking the Blockchain*, ed. R. Catlow, M. Garrett, N. Jones, and S. Skinner. Liverpool: Liverpool University Press.

Christensen, C. 2016. *The Innovator's Dilemma: When New Technologies Cause Great Firms to Fail*. Boston: Harvard Business Review Press.

De Filippi, P., G. McMullen, T. McConaghy, C. Choi, S. de la Rouviere, J. Benet, and D. Stern. 2016. How Blockchains Can Support, Complement, or Supplement Intellectual Property: Working Draft, Version 1.0, COALA. http://docplayer.net/56177308-How-blockchains-can-support-complement-or-supplement-intellectual-property.html. Accessed 4 May 2018.

De Filippi, P., and A. Wright. 2018. *Blockchain and the Law: The Rule of Code*. Cambridge, MA: Harvard University Press.
De Vries, A. 2018. Bitcoin's Growing Energy Problem. *Joule*. https://www.cell.com/joule/fulltext/S2542-4351(18)30177-6. Accessed 23 June 2018.
Digiconomist. 2018. Bitcoin Energy Consumption Index. https://digiconomist.net/bitcoin-energy-consumption. Accessed 27 June 2018.
Dodd, N. 2017. The Social Life of Bitcoin. *Theory, Culture and Society* 35: 35–56.
Elsden, C., A. Manohar, J. Briggs, M. Harding, C. Speed, and J. Vines. 2018. Making Sense of Blockchain Applications: A Typology for HCI. In *Proceedings of the 2018 CHI Conference*, 21–26, April, Montreal. https://chriselsden.files.wordpress.com/2018/01/elsden-making-sense-of-blockchain-applications.pdf. Accessed 4 May 2018.
FCA. 2017. Regulatory Sandbox Lessons Learned Report. https://www.fca.org.uk/publication/research-and-data/regulatory-sandbox-lessons-learned-report.pdf. Accessed 28 June 2018.
Fintech Times. 2018. Malta on Best Track to Become a Blockchain Hub. http://thefintechtimes.com/malta-on-best-track-to-become-a-blockchain-hub/. Accessed 27 June 2018.
Golumbia, D. 2016. *The Politics of Bitcoin: Software as Right-Wing Extremism*. Minneapolis: University of Minnesota Press.
Greenfield, A. 2017. *Radical Technologies: The Design of Everyday Life*. London and New York: Verso.
Holmes, C. 2017. Distributed Ledger Technologies for Public Good: Leadership, Collaboration and Innovation. http://chrisholmes.co.uk/wp-content/uploads/2017/11/Distributed-Ledger-Technologies-for-Public-Good_leadership-collaboration-and-innovation.pdf. Accessed 2 March 2018.
Howard, G. 2017. *Everything in Its Right Place: How Blockchain Technology Will Lead to a More Transparent Music Industry*. Beverly Farms, MA: 9GiantSteps.
Howkins, J. 2007. *The Creative Economy*, updated edition. London: Penguin.
Huckle, S., and M. White. 2016. Socialism and the Blockchain. *Future Internet* 8 (4): 49–63.
Kranzberg, M. 1995. Technology and History: 'Kranzberg's Laws'. *Bulletin of Science, Technology & Society* 15 (1): 5–13.
Lam. 2017. 'Where are the Women in the Blockchain Network?'. *Forbes*. https://www.forbes.com/sites/lamjackie/2017/12/10/where-are-the-women-in-the-blockchain-network/. Accessed 13 September 2018.
McAfee, A., and E. Brynjolfsson. 2017. *Machine Platform Crowd: Harnessing Our Digital Future*. New York and London: Norton.
Murphy, H. 2018. 'Bitcoin Whales' Control Third of Market with $37.5bn Holdings. *Financial Times*. https://amp-ft-com.cdn.ampproject.org/c/s/amp.ft.com/content/c4b68aec-6b26-11e8-8cf3-0c230fa67aec. Accessed 23 June 2018.

Myers, R. 2017. Blockchain Poetics. In *Artists Re: Thinking the Blockchain*, ed. R. Catlow, M. Garrett, N. Jones, and S. Skinner. Liverpool: Liverpool University Press.

Nadal, M., and C.E. Andaluz. 2017. Critical Mining: Blockchain and Bitcoin in Contemporary Art. In *Artists Re:Thinking the Blockchain*, ed. R. Catlow, M. Garrett, N. Jones, and S. Skinner. Liverpool: Liverpool University Press.

Narayanan, A., J. Bonneau, E. Felten, A. Miller, and S. Goldfeder. 2016. *Bitcoin and Cryptocurrency Technologies: A Comprehensive Introduction*. Princeton and Oxford: Princeton University Press.

O'Dwyer, R. 2017. Blockchains and Their Pitfalls. In *Ours to Hack and to Own: The Rise of Platform Co-operativism, a New Vision for the Future of Work and a Fairer Internet*, ed. T. Scholz and N. Schneider. New York: OR Books.

O'Dwyer, K., and D. Malone. 2014. Bitcoin Mining and Its Energy Footprint. ISSC 2014/ CIICT 14. Limerick, 26–27 June. http://karlodwyer.com/publications/pdf/bitcoin_KJOD_2014.pdf. Accessed 4 May 2018.

Parks, L., and N. Starosielski. 2015. Introduction. In *Signal Traffic: Critical Studies of Media Infrastructures*, ed. L. Parks and N. Starosielski. Urbana, Chicago: University of Illinois Press.

PWC. 2017. Introduction to Token Sales (ICO) Best Practices. https://www.pwccn.com/en/financial-services/publications/introduction-to-token-sales-ico-best-practices.pdf. Accessed 2 March 2018.

Rossiter, N. 2016. *Software, Infrastructure, Labour: A Media Theory of Logistical Nightmares*. London: Routledge.

Scherbin, A. 2018. Best Countries for ICO. https://hackernoon.com/best-countries-for-ico-ef710ace2785. Accessed 27 June 2018.

Schroff, S., and J. Street. 2017. The Politics of the Digital Single Market: Culture vs. Competition vs. Copyright. *Information, Communication & Society*. https://www.tandfonline.com/doi/abs/10.1080/1369118X.2017.1309445. Accessed 8 May 2018.

Tapscott D., and A. Tapscott. 2017. *Realising the Potential of Blockchain: A Multistakeholder Approach to the Stewardship of Blockchain and Cryptocurrencies*. World Economic Forum. http://www3.weforum.org/docs/WEF_Realizing_Potential_Blockchain.pdf. Accessed 10 November 2017.

Tapscott, D., and A. Tapscott. 2018. Who Would Win the World Cup of Blockchain? *Quartz*. https://qz.com/1315302/who-would-win-the-world-cup-of-blockchain/. Accessed 27 June 2018.

Tasca, P. 2015. Digital Currencies: Principles, Trend, Opportunities, Risks. https://papers.ssrn.com/sol3/Papers.cfm?abstract_id=2657598. Accessed 4 May 2018.

Tasca, P., T. Thayabaran, and C. Tessone. 2017. Ontology of Blockchain Technologies: Principles of Identification and Classification. https://papers.ssrn.com/sol3/papers.cfm?abstract_id=2977811. Accessed 25 August 2017.

Thompson, C. 2017. How to Do an Initial Coin Offering (Part 1). https://medium.com/blockchain-review/how-to-do-an-ico-d02c54a990c2. Accessed 27 June 2018.

Wright, A., and P. De Filippi. 2015. Decentralised Blockchain Technology and the Rise of Lex Cryptographia. https://papers.ssrn.com/sol3/papers.cfm?abstract_id=2580664. Accessed 2 March 2018.

Zeilinger, M. 2016. Digital Art as 'Monetised Graphics': Enforcing Intellectual Property on the Blockchain. *Philosophy & Technology* 31 (1): 15–41.

Zetzsche, D., Buckley, R., and D. Arner. 2017. The Distributed Liability of Distributed Ledgers: Legal Risks of Blockchain. Law Working Paper Series, Number 2017-007. University of New South Wales Law Research Series.

CHAPTER 6

Conclusion and Recommendations

Abstract While the internet 1.0 has benefitted users more than it has benefitted artists, the internet 2.0 (also known as web 3.0) has tremendous potential for creators. Start-ups in the space understand this, as do some creators and a growing number of incumbents. Now policy-makers need to understand the potential—and the potential risks of inaction. At present, we are in danger of blockchain start-ups gravitating to countries other than the UK—resulting in a significant loss of economic and cultural value. At the same time, as outlined in the previous chapter, there are signifiant risks associated with blockchain technology, which policy-makers have a duty to address. This chapter contains seven recommendations for the UK Government. Yet this is not an issue for policy-makers alone. Representatives of both start-ups and established organisations need to work with policy-makers—not least as a way to prevent unhelpful regulation. Regulation, after all, occurs not only through law but also through code, social norms and market economics. Since blockchain is a genuinely disruptive technology, the market economics ultimately favour new entrants rather than established organisations. Intermediaries will not disappear but they will be obliged to re-invent themselves if they wish to survive in a potentially distributed future.

Keywords Blockchain call to action · Value gap · Blockchain policy recommendations · Blockchain futures · Disruptive technology

M. O'Dair, *Distributed Creativity*,
https://doi.org/10.1007/978-3-030-00190-2_6

Castells (2010) states that the network society—which is based on the internet, or what Tapscott and Tapscott (2017) call the internet 1.0—is strikingly unequal:

> While everything and everybody on the planet felt the effects of this new social structure, global networks included some people and territories while excluding others, so inducing a geography of social, economic and technological inequality. (Castells 2010, p. xviii)

Similarly, Ferguson (2017) argues that the technological revolution of the internet has been followed by commercialisation and the rise of monopolies and duopolies. The success of Microsoft, Apple, Facebook, Google, and Amazon, Ferguson suggests, present us with a paradox: 'The world is connected as never before, as the cheerleaders of these companies never tire of saying. Yet the world is (in some respects) unequal as it has not been for a century' (p. 357). The tension between distributed networks and hierarchical orders, for Ferguson, 'is as old as humanity itself' (p. 425).

Blockchain technology, argue Tapscott and Tapscott (2017), represents the internet 2.0. Some prefer to conceptualise the new era as web 3.0. Either way, the point is that this time it could be different, because this time it could be decentralised. Certainly, a number of myths have sprung up to accompany the hype: that blockchains are entirely 'trustless', that they are immutable, that they are 100% secure, and that they are 'trust machines'. In fact, as Hileman and Rauchs (2017, pp. 17–18) argue, blockchains always require some degree of trust, even if only in the underlying cryptography. Blockchain transactions can also be reversed in certain circumstances; blockchains are not automatically more secure than other systems; and the 'garbage in, garbage out' problem applies to every blockchain that uses non-native digital assets and/or external data inputs (Hileman and Rauchs 2017, pp. 17–18). Yet this is nonetheless a potentially transformative—and, as Tapscott and Tapscott (2018) suggest, even a revolutionary—technology. The question is whether or not that potential will be realised, since no technology is worth much if it doesn't get adopted, and what the effects—negative as well as positive—will be if it is.

It is early days: 'in terms of its ecology of tools and infrastructures,' argues Catlow (2017, p. 24), 'the blockchain is at the same stage of development as the WWW [World Wide Web] in the early 90s.' Of those I interviewed for this book, Phil Barry expects mainstream adoption within twelve months, but others (Bryce Bladon, Robert Norton, Josef Marc) expect to wait a few years. It does not seem over-optimistic, however, to state that the use of blockchains could be everyday within five-to-ten years, within the creative economy and beyond—although, as Phil Barry points out in our interview, users may not be aware that they are using a blockchain at all. Although this book has focused on start-ups, incumbents have also begun to adopt the technology. To take the music industry alone, we have seen Spotify's acquisition of Mediachain, a blockchain-start-up, in 2017, and, the same year, news of a blockchain initiative from the collection societies PRS for Music, SACEM and ASCAP. In fact, these developments may not be particularly significant in themselves, but they represent, at least, a new willingness to engage with the technology. Those who purchased Björk's 2017 album, *Utopia*, were rewarded with a cryptocurrency, audiocoin, that is intended as a means of rewarding fans for sharing links to tour dates, merchandise and so on. In 2018, JAAK revealed details of a collaboration with large music organisations including Warner Music Group, one of the three major record labels. Blokur, meanwhile, are working with one of the world's largest music publishers. And Dot Blockchain Media, a New York-based start-up founded by music entrepreneur Benji Rogers, have partnered with the Canadian collecting society SOCAN as well as other established music organisations. Innovation may typically begin in the margins, but blockchain is fast moving centre stage. The need to get this right, then, is urgent, and it will require collaboration between multiple stakeholders, from creators to policy-makers. Below, I set out the reasons why work needs to begin immediately, before concluding with seven recommendations.

Reasons to Act

The internet 1.0 has benefitted users more than it has benefitted artists. The status quo is not working for creators, due to major challenges posed by attribution; data silos; slow, inefficient and opaque royalty payments; and difficulties in licensing. The result is known, in the music industry, as the value gap (IFPI 2017): the sky-high levels of consumption that characterise the streaming are not being matched by fair returns to creators. Blockchain technology could be integral to solving these problems, as well as in setting parameters for the pricing and usage of tickets and creative works. Blockchains can also unlock the value of distributed ownership, consumption data, digital scarcity, smart *droit de suite* payments and tokens. Blockchain needs to be taken seriously as a technology with creative economy (and not only fintech) applications. Bazalgette (2017, p. 35) has already noted that blockchains could 'revolutionise' the sector. Start-ups understand this, as do some creators, notably the musicians Björk and Imogen Heap, and the artist Jonas Lund, who has released a token that allows holders to vote on issues concerning his creative practice. Established organisations are starting to wake up too. Policy-makers need to join them. We are told that 'the UK has a dual competitive advantage in creative and technological skills and our future prosperity will be driven by this particular combination of strengths' (DCMS 2018). Yet the creative economy is neglected in both the Walport report (2016) on blockchain and distributed ledger technology and the follow-up by Holmes (2017).

If policy-makers do not get this right, there is a danger that blockchain companies in the creative economy and beyond will favour counties other than the UK. Start-ups using blockchain technologies, as Casey and Vigna (2018, p. 255) note, gravitate to friendly jurisdictions such as 'crypto valley' in Switzerland. This would represent a significant loss of economic, as well as cultural value; the creative economy is acknowledged as 'at the heart of the UK's competitive advantage' and a 'major strategic opportunity' for export (HM Government 2018). Failure to attract blockchain companies working in the creative economy would also lead to a decline in soft power, an area of traditional strength (Young and Cauldwell-French 2018). The imminence of Brexit makes the 'soft power' point particularly important (HM Government , p. 9). Certainly, there are some bad actors in the space, and consumers require protection. Yet anyone seeking to regulate cryptocurrencies and tokens needs to be extremely careful not to pour cold water on a whole wave of DLT innovation. As Burke et al. state:

> Nations around the globe are in the process of waking up to the economic and technological opportunities and challenges that this [blockchain and distributed ledger technologies] offers their economies. Approaches vary from an outright ban (e.g.: China who sees digital money as a threat to their attempts to restrict capital outflow) to a broadly positive environment in a number of jurisdictions aiming to become global financial hubs: Switzerland, Singapore, Estonia, Malta and centres of technological innovation such as France… Regulators need to be wary of the flight of intellectual and human capital as much as they worry about losing monetary gains with regulations

> that lag innovation occurring in the token ecosystem. Tokenised start-ups and the companies that service them are often made up of distributed teams and are highly mobile. Where governments have been unfriendly to token-based innovations, those have been quick to resettle in more welcoming jurisdictions. Japan saw an influx of blockchain start-ups after the China ban, Binance, one of the largest crypto-asset exchanges, moved from Hong Kong to Malta and Indian entrepreneurs have begun moving towards Singapore as a response to the Reserve Bank of India requesting local banks avoid catering to token-based businesses. In fact, even the US and its highly prized Silicon Valley ecosystem has become concerned in the light of the SECs inconsistent and often ambiguous communications around tokens. So much so its leading venture capitalists recently joined forces to lobby the SEC to offer a non-exclusive safe harbour to good actors, specifically citing the outflow of talent as a threat to their industries future. (Burke et al. 2018)

At the same time, representatives of the creative economy need to work *with* policy-makers and regulators. Regulating an unpermissioned ledger is challenging, to say the least; some would say it is impossible, although it should be feasible to regulate wallet providers and exchanges. Bryce Bladon states in our interview that the CryptoKitties team worked with regulators prior to launch. It was, Bladon concedes, a time-consuming process, but he also describes it as the best way to deliver a positive outcome for both parties, as well as for CryptoKitties users. This will be anathema to cypherpunks, and there is likely be a tension here between disruptive/radical and sustaining/incorporative applications (even if the lines sometimes blur, as disruptive/radical start-ups pair up with corporates pursuing a more sustaining/incorporative agenda). Whether cryptocurrency users like it or not, however, blockchains have come a long way since Nakamoto's (2008) white paper, with banks (the very institutions bitcoin was supposed to cut out) and tech giants such as IBM now firmly on board, and enterprise applications of the technology are inconceivable without a proactive approach to engaging with policy-makers and regulators. It is only through dialogue that a sensible, light-touch approach to regulation is going to be achieved, avoiding the sort of heavy-handed bans we have seen in some countries. Crucially, regulation does not need to be carried out only by those we traditionally think of as regulators. Lessig (2006) argues that there are *four* regulators in any given space: law, social norms, market economics and technological architecture. Blockchain maximalists are wrong to interpret Lessig's words as meaning that we need only code; at the same time, those in favour of increased regulation need to understand that changes to the law are only one means of achieving a given end. Code, market economics and social norms all have important roles too. Not all solutions need to be centralised; communities of users can play a vital role in red-flagging bad actors in the world of token sales, for instance. Not all the challenges—scalability, for instance—are for policy-makers to solve. Introducing new policies is also very slow; on the whole, what is required is guidance as to how existing regulation should be interpreted.

Working with policy-makers and regulators would help overcome some barriers to adoption. It is also key if we are to overcome some of the risks I identify in Chapter 5. Blockchains, for instance, could be used to illegally store large volumes of creative works beyond the reach of notice and takedown procedures. This loss of control over copyrighted works is one of the threats identified by De Filippi and Wright (2018), and it would make the situation facing creators and their industry representatives worse rather than better. De Filippi and Wright also identify the opposite threat: that blockchains could be used to introduce a new form of digital rights management, which might be good for large rights holders but not for creators—or fans. We would do well to remember Kranzberg's first law (1995).

Recommendations

Below are seven recommendations for policy-makers, primarily those in the UK. On the whole, they concern blockchain technology in general terms; at this early stage, it seems more appropriate to ensure that the creative economy is an integral part of the development of that technology, rather than to make specific recommendations for creative economy applications. Those may become appropriate later, as the ecosystem matures. One general point is that policy-makers should consider disruptive/radical blockchain applications of the technology, not only sustaining/incorporative ones, and should not confine themselves to the permissioned, private systems that are so often the focus of government interest in this space. Blockchain technology emerged as a bottom-up, rather than top-down phenomenon, and that—rather than improvements in efficiency—remains the application with the most potential for innovation. Some of the recommended actions could be carried out immediately, while others are longer term.

Recommendation 1: Embed Blockchain Technology in the Industrial Strategy and Creative Industries 'Sector Deal'

The UK Government appears to prioritise artificial intelligence (AI) and immersive technologies in its Industrial Strategy (2017)—despite referencing in that document the Bazalgette report (2017), which states explicitly that blockchain technology could revolutionise the creative industries. Blockchains are mentioned *once* in the 256 pages of the Industrial Strategy; distributed ledger technology is not mentioned at all. On the other hand, AI (with big data) is one of the four 'grand challenges' identified as a priority, and the Industrial Strategy also commits to investing £33 million in immersive technologies. Blockchain technology is not mentioned *at all* in the recent creative industries sector deal drawn up by the UK Government (2018), despite the fact that one pillar of that sector deal is a commitment to tackle copyright infringement and close the value gap. By contrast, the sector deal refers to £58 million for immersive technologies and commits to doubling the UK's share of the global creative immersive content market by 2025. Blockchain is every bit as important as other 'fourth industrial revolution' (Schwab 2016) technologies; for Tapscott and Tapscott (2017), blockchain is in fact 'the foundational platform' of that revolution. This should not be seen as a competition between technologies: the full potential of the fourth industrial revolution lies in technological *convergence* (Lundy et al. 2018). Yet blockchain technology is certainly of considerable importance since, as outlined in Chapter 3, it has the potential to unlock enormous value in the creative economy and beyond. It needs to become a strategic priority alongside immersive technologies and AI—and its specific potential for the creative economy also needs to be recognised.

Recommendation 2: Establish a Cross-Sector, Cross-Departmental Blockchain Working Group to Co-ordinate Pilot Projects and Share Best Practice

The publication of the Walport report in 2016 established the UK as a thought-leading blockchain nation. As Lord Holmes (2017) acknowledges, much of this momentum has been lost. There are valuable blockchain and distributed ledger technology committees and working groups, for instance at techUK and BSI (full disclosure: I am a member of both). We also have groups such as the British Blockchain Association, as well as the Blockchain All-Party Parliamentary Group and, most recently, the Crypto-assets

Taskforce. Numerous Government departments also have an interest in the area, from the Department for International Development to HM Revenue and Customs, and there have even been a number of pilots, from the Food Standards Agency to the Department for Work and Pensions. Yet the work of these groups is siloed; paradoxically, given the nature of the technology concerned, it is centralised. And at the same time, exciting initiatives such as the Blockchain Observatory are being launched in the European Union—just as the UK prepares to leave in the wake of the Brexit referendum. From Estonia to Dubai, ambitious plans to integrate blockchain into government are not only being talked about but actually being put into practice. What is required in the UK now is a group that is cross-government (albeit managed by one department, most likely the Cabinet Office) and cross-sector. Again, there is a potential template in the UK's approach to AI. A senior civil servant could be tasked with co-ordinating blockchain activity across the civil service. DCMS (Department for Digital, Culture, Media, and Sport) should take the lead by establishing a task force, with involvement from BEIS (Department for Business, Energy and Industrial Strategy), and the Government Digital Service could head up cross-departmental applications. That DCMS is the obvious champion for such an initiative is good news for the creative economy, with media and culture falling under the same departmental brief as digital. With the creative economy in mind, in particular the sector deal promise to tackle copyright infringement, the involvement of the Intellectual Property Office is also critical. The working group should study the approaches adopted by countries such as Switzerland, and develop a blockchain code of practice that would 'professionalise the industry and educate investors sufficiently to stop most scam coin activity' (Taylor 2017). An excellent starting point is the code of conduct developed by Global Digital Finance (2018), an industry body dedicated to accelerating the adoption of digital finance technologies. Finally, the working group should take a lead on co-ordinating the Government's blockchain pilots, reporting on progress and sharing best practice. Ultimately, blockchain technology could lead to significant savings for the UK Government. It could also bring about something much more transformative: a whole new governmental architecture.

Recommendation 3: Extend the Sandbox Programme to Include Tokens, 'Green' Consensus Mechanisms and Industries Beyond Fintech

Blockchain companies are attracted to Zug, in Switzerland, because of a relatively favourable legal and regulatory environment, note Casey and

Vigna (2018, p. 255). Casey and Vigna also point out the success of the FCA sandbox as a means of encouraging innovation in the UK. 'Sandbox' can be a vague term but the FCA sandbox set—and met—four specific aims: to reduce the time and cost of getting innovative ideas to market; to enable greater access to finance by reducing regulatory uncertainty; to enable more products to be tested and potentially introduced to the market; and to allow the FCA to work with innovators to ensure that appropriate consumer protection safeguards were built into new products and services (FCA 2017). What is required now is for the FCA to extend the sandbox programme, for instance to examine the opportunities and challenges relating to tokens. Even those start-ups not issuing tokens would benefit from greater professionalisation of tokens, since bad practice—accompanied by widespread hype—currently threatens the credibility of blockchain technology more broadly. Something broader is also required, going beyond the remit of the FCA: the sandbox concept needs to be extended to sectors far beyond financial services, for instance the creative industries, and there needs to be a particular effort to encourage more ecologically-friendly approaches to achieving consensus.

Recommendation 4: Publish Clear Guidelines on the Treatment of Cryptocurrencies and Tokens

As I stated in Chapter 4, cryptocurrencies operate in a legal grey area. The same is true of tokens. Clear guidelines would help to bring clarity; to paraphrase Andy Grant of Artos, start-ups would then at least know the rules of the game. Irina Albita, Maria Tanjala, and Jamie Sly from FilmChain also call, in our interview, for the Government to draft a clear regulatory framework for launching and scaling blockchain companies. Certainly, there is more to blockchain technology than token sales, and the majority of the respondents interviewed for this book are not issuing tokens at all. Yet this subject is of interest even to blockchain companies not utilising tokens, since bad actors running scam token sales are discrediting the entire space. At present, the lack of clarity is making the UK unattractive for companies that do issue tokens: of the 2000 token sales examined as of 1 July 2018 by TokenIntelligence.io, a leading token analytics platform, less than 2% are domiciled in the UK (Barry James, 2018, personal communication).

Firstly, these guidelines should clearly state which crypto investments are subject to taxation. The USA, for instance, has recently closed a tax loophole, meaning that capital gains tax must be paid on profits from cryptocurrency trades. Secondly, the guidelines should explain what is considered a utility token and what a security—and differentiate cryptocurrencies from either. Regulation, otherwise, will be a very blunt tool. America has the Howey test for securities, named after a 1946 case in the Supreme Court; recently, America's Securities and Exchange Commission (SEC) even launched Howeycoins, a fake token sale intended to educate investors and alert them to potential scams. Abu Dhabi has also issued guidelines for token sales. In the UK, the FCA has said that it will approach each token sale on a case-by-case basis. While this position has a certain logic, since some tokens are akin to securities while others resemble a new form of crowdfunding, it does not do much to promote business and consumer confidence. Clear guidelines on the UK Government's attitude towards all crypto-assets would help make the UK attractive to blockchain businesses, including those in the creative economy.

Publishing clear guidelines, to be sure, is far easier said than done. At the same time, as Burke et al. argue

> Lawyers look to the jurisdiction which can best reduce risk and protect their issuing clients. Globally, a huge amount of uncertainty still exists around the future, and even retrospective treatment, of crypto-assets and cryptocurrencies. No major world economy has yet taken the step to provide absolute certainty as to the treatment of an ICO that does not represent a 'security'. This would ideally include guidance on which existing regulations should apply to this new class of assets, where new regulation is required and its timeline, as well as a consultation process with industry on its design. (Burke et al. 2018)

Again, the efforts of Global Digital Finance (2018) to establish 'a consistent and reliable crypto-asset taxonomy' are highly relevant here. Also relevant is the paper on the application of securities laws, as they relate to tokens, published by the Monetary Authority of Singapore (2017). In the UK, the newly established Crypto-assets Taskforce—a collaboration between HM Treasury, the Bank of England and the FCA—is the obvious candidate for the job.

Recommendation 5: Establish Blockchain Innovation Hubs Around the UK

Blockchain start-ups require more than a decent business model and some good developers. To be successful, they need to consider a whole range of issues that are beyond the remit of the typical entrepreneur. At this early stage, it is even difficult for some start-ups to find credible advisors. Tokens alone, for instance, take start-ups into a whole range of potentially new areas, from behavioural economics to law. Dan Fowler of JAAK alludes to this in our interview:

> *O'Dair*: What do you consider the risks – to your company and beyond – of adopting blockchain technology? Again, please consider political, economic, social, technological, legal and/or environmental factors.
>
> *Fowler*: Blockchain technology is nascent, and building decentralised infrastructure is difficult. Things will break, and so there is an increased emphasis on the requirement for redundancy and robust design. The overarching regulatory environment and crypto investment backdrop are evolving. This requires projects to invest in areas that might not be a typical priority for equivalent teams developing centralised technology.

What is required is a series of hubs, around the UK, providing specialist support for blockchain start-ups—not only in fintech but also, for instance, in the creative economy. As Burke et al. (2018) state, we need 'a proactive policy to encourage innovation and jobs in the UK,' which could involve 'the provision of support via bodies such as Digital Catapult.' Given the environmental impact of proof-of-work consensus mechanisms as they currently operate, these hubs should promote the development of proof-of-stake and other less ecologically harmful approaches to achieving consensus. These hubs could also help to educate businesses (since start-ups, as Dan Fowler suggests, currently have to spend time dispelling blockchain myths) and creators (who may not be aware of the opportunities I examine in Chapter 3, nor the risks I examine in Chapter 5). Embedding blockchain technology in the Industrial Strategy (see above) will make it easier to fund such an initiative; private funding could also be sought, for instance for partnerships between universities and business clusters. It may also be that some of the £20 million committed, in the creative industries sector deal, to supporting creative centres across the country could be channelled in this direction. The initiative could also be linked to the Tech Nation programme, through which the Government has already pledged money to support regional tech hubs around the UK.

Recommendation 6: Invest in the Blockchain Talent Pipeline Through Schools and Universities

As I mention in Chapter 4, the need for more blockchain developers is acute. While blockchain jobs are estimated to have increased by over 200% in 2017, blockchain developers are in short supply—to the extent that they are able to charge up to $200 an hour (Burke et al. 2018). While blockchain hubs should help in the short term, what is required to support the blockchain ecosystem in the longer term is investment in developers—as well as lawyers, behavioural economists and creative economy representatives—with advanced knowledge of blockchain technology. Such an initiative, closely linked to embedding blockchain in the Industrial Strategy (see above), should also help to overcome the lack of diversity noted in Chapter 5. The imminence of Brexit only makes the issue more urgent, since the UK is relatively weak in terms of governmental support and funding for blockchain technology. The UK Government is committed to plugging the AI skills gap; why does blockchain not receive the same treatment?

A portion of the £406 million dedicated, in the Industrial Strategy, to additional maths, digital and technical education should go towards blockchain and distributed ledger technology. Yet support should not be excusive to STEM (Science, Technology, Engineering, Mathematics) subjects but should extend to a range of sectors, including those related to the creative economy. As Christine Mohan states in our interview, students on liberal arts programmes need to learn about blockchain technology too. And while investing in schools would be a very positive step, it would take years to see the benefits. In the shorter term, it will be better to establish doctoral training centres—either for blockchain technology specifically or, perhaps, for distributed systems more broadly, with a particular focus on 'greener' alternatives to proof-of-work consensus mechanisms as they currently stand. Irina Albita, Maria Tanjala and Jamie Sly from FilmChain state in our interview that they would welcome collaboration between government and universities. Burke et al. (2018) call for budget to upskill and train for in-demand technology roles via engagement with universities; the AI sector deal for training and Ph.D. sponsorship, as they point out, is a useful reference point in terms of how this might work in practice.

Recommendation 7: Take the Lead in Working Towards Global, Multi-Stakeholder Blockchain Governance

As I state in Chapter 4, regional and national approaches to a globally distributed ledger can only ever be partially effective. That different countries have different approaches to cryptocurrencies and tokens is a significant challenge for companies deploying blockchain technology. Andy Grant of Artos spoke, in our interview, of the need for a worldwide consortium engaged with governments around the world. Tapscott and Tapscott (2017) have written in more detail about what such a multi-stakeholder approach to blockchain stewardship might look like, comprising networked institutions, standards networks, advocacy networks, policy and watchdog networks, delivery networks and knowledge networks. As they state:

> We cannot leave governance of such complex global innovations solely either to governments or to the private sector: political and commercial interests have proven insufficient to ensure that this new resource serves society. Rather, and more than ever, we need multi-stakeholders to collaborate as equals and provide global leadership. We need all three pillars of modern civilisation – the private sector, the public sector and civil society – to participate in stewarding this new global resource. (Tapscott and Tapscott 2017, p. 28)

Global, multi-stakeholder governance for blockchain technology is, admittedly, an ambitious goal, but it is also a very worthwhile one—not least because it would help create standards and interoperability, reducing the risk of simply building new silos on the internet 2.0. This is an opportunity for the UK to take a lead and establish itself as a leading blockchian nation. Following the Walport (2016) and Holmes (2017) reports, as well as the successful FCA sandbox, we already have a head start. The country already has a reasonably high number of blockchain start-ups, and London is firmly established as a global centre of banking and commerce. The UK also is also renowned for its blockchain research. Yet this lead is beginning to slide. That the UK is one of the countries to have recently signed up to the European Blockchain Partnership is a good start but there is further to go—not least in looking beyond Europe. We should, at the very least, be at the forefront of work in the area by groups such as the Organisation for Economic Co-operation and Development (OECD).

The Future Is Distributed

Blockchain technology offers huge potential to the creative economy and beyond but it also poses significant risks. The technology also faces significant barriers to adoption. From a technological perspective, for instance, many organisations are now reliant upon ethereum—yet ethereum can still be brought to its knees by too many people playing CryptoKitties. Yet it is growing at an impressive pace. 'Blockless' distributed ledger technologies (such as directed acyclic graphs) are emerging too, and may supersede blockchains altogether. For established organisations in the creative economy, burying heads in the sand is not a sensible option; nor is trying to close blockchain down. Both approaches were attempted by the music industry when presented by a previous generation of peer-to-peer networks and the lessons are informative. The big players in the music industry, as represented by the Recording Industry Association of America, might have won against Napster, but they lost against every other 'pirate' platform that followed—and the reason they lost is that these second-generation networks were decentralised. Blockchain technology takes that decentralisation to a whole new level. There are all kinds of barriers, and adoption, which will certainly be slower than technological determinists predict, is by no means inevitable. But it is at the very least entirely feasible, and so we should prepare. If decentralised technologies do not necessarily decentralise power, then the question of who is involved in building this new architecture is critically important; incumbents need to think about working *with* blockchains, and to do so fast. Policy-makers also need to act as a matter of urgency, to maximise opportunities and minimise risks, since several other countries are already making bold strides and the UK is falling behind. The challenge is to do so without restricting innovation.

For the creative economy, the appeal of blockchain technology is that it could lead towards a world in which creators can be inextricably linked to their creative works; in which IP data is stored in distributed rather than centralised (and conflicting) databases; and in which payments and licensing are automated through smart contracts. Blockchains place creators, for the first time, in the centre of the creative economy: Imogen Heap, for instance, is working towards issuing all musicians, and potentially other creators, with 'creative passports through her Mycelia initiative. We are looking at a game-changing opportunity for creators to take ownership of their data—and, therefore, their whole careers. While bitcoin prices and token sales grab the headlines, blockchain technology is not merely a new speculative asset or source of start-up finance. It affects entire business models and, indeed, entire value systems. In fact, the less reputable token sales, for instance those held by companies whose business models remain dubious or unarticulated, may harm the ecosystem, at least in the short term. The fact that we may now be in a 'trough of disappointment,' as the potential of blockchain technology is realised more slowly than some expected, is no reason to write off the whole technology: over-estimating short-term impact of new technologies is as common as under-estimating their impact in the longer term. Hype, and corresponding blockchain fatigue, is itself a barrier to adoption. It is important to acknowledge that there are, at least at the present moment, a number of things that blockchains cannot do (Tucker and Catalini 2018). It is also essential to keep in mind, however, that blockchains are a genuinely disruptive technology—and disruptive technologies, as Bower and Christensen (1995) have shown, have a particular performance trajectory (the rate at which their performance improves over time). Disruptive technologies often fare worse than sustaining technologies when measured in terms of attributes traditionally valued by mainstream customers. The crucial point, for Bower and Christensen, is that this simply does not matter: what is significant is the performance trajectory of the disruptive technology *compared with that of the market*. Due to their entrenched value systems, established organisations often fail to realise this until it is too late—hence the co-called innovator's dilemma (Christensen 2016). Those incumbents wondering whether or not blockchain technology will affect the creative economy, then, are asking the wrong question. The real question is: if blockchains, or other distributed ledger technologies, are adopted, will they transform the creative economy for good or ill? Different stakeholders will have very different answers.

The rigid value systems of established organisations, coupled with the attacker's advantage enjoyed by new entrants, make the creative industries—like numerous other industries—ripe for disintermediation. Yet this is by no means to say that every intermediary will disappear. True, the ingenuity of bitcoin lies in 'allowing any two willing parties to transact directly with each other without the need for a trusted third party' (Nakamoto 2008, p. 1) and blockchain technology does pose a threat to intermediaries (Godsiff 2016). Yet transaction cost economics and the impossibility of complete contracts suggest that we are going to see a thinning of middlemen and women rather than their complete removal from the value system (McAfee and Brynjolfsson 2017). Intermediaries that add value will remain—and, of course, new intermediaries will emerge too. Established organisations will, however, need to re-invent themselves. The point made by Howkins (2007) still holds: businesses, and indeed entire industries, do not collapse because their business models become outdated. They collapse because they fail to find new ones.

References

Bazalgette, P. 2017. Independent Review of the Creative Industries. https://assets.publishing.service.gov.uk/government/uploads/system/uploads/attachment_data/file/649980/Independent_Review_of_the_Creative_Industries.pdf. Accessed 2 May 2017.

Bower, J., and C. Christensen. 1995. Disruptive Technologies: Catching the Wave. *Harvard Business Review*. https://hbr.org/1995/01/disruptive-technologies-catching-the-wave. Accessed 29 June 2018.

Burke, J., M. Law, J. Roberts, J. John, and C. Thomas. 2018. Evidence Submission to the Treasury Committee Inquiry into Digital Currencies. https://outlierventures.io/research/evidence-submission-to-the-treasury-committee-inquiry-into-digital-currencies/. Accessed 1 July.

Casey, M., and P. Vigna. 2018. *The Truth Machine: The Blockchain and the Future of Everything*. London: Harper Collins.

Castells, M. 2010. *The Rise of the Network Society. The Information Age: Economy, Society and Culture*, vol. 1, 2nd ed. Oxford: Wiley-Blackwell.

Catlow, R. 2017. Artists Re:Thinking the Blockchain Introduction. In *Artists Re:Thinking the Blockchain*, ed. R. Catlow, M. Garrett, N. Jones, and S. Skinner. Liverpool: Liverpool University Press.

Christensen, C. 2016. *The Innovator's Dilemma: When New Technologies Cause Great Firms to Fail*. Boston: Harvard Business Review Press.

DCMS. 2018. Culture Is Digital. https://www.gov.uk/government/publications/culture-is-digital/culture-is-digital. Accessed 2 May 2018.

De Filippi, P., and A. Wright. 2018. *Blockchain and the Law: The Rule of Code*. Cambridge, MA: Harvard University Press.

FCA. 2017. Regulatory Sandbox Lessons Learned Report. https://www.fca.org.uk/publication/research-and-data/regulatory-sandbox-lessons-learned-report.pdf. Accessed 28 June 2018.

Ferguson, N. 2017. *The Square and the Tower: Networks, Hierarchies and the Struggle for Global Power*. London: Penguin.

Global Digital Finance. 2018. https://www.gdf.io. Accessed 1 July 2018.

Godsiff, P. 2016. Disruptive Potential. In *Distributed Ledger Technology: Beyond Blockchain*, ed. M. Walport. https://www.gov.uk/government/uploads/system/uploads/attachment_data/le/492972/gs-16-1-distributed-ledger-technology.pdf. Accessed 24 October 2017.

HM Government. 2017. Industrial Strategy: Building a Britain Fit for the Future. https://assets.publishing.service.gov.uk/government/uploads/system/uploads/attachment_data/file/664563/industrial-strategy-white-paper-web-ready-version.pdf. Accessed 13 September 2018.

HM Government. 2018. Industrial Strategy: Creative Industries Sector Deal. https://assets.publishing.service.gov.uk/government/uploads/system/uploads/attachment_data/file/695097/creative-industries-sector-deal-print.pdf. Accessed 29 June 2018.

Hileman, G., and M. Rauchs. 2017. Global Blockchain Benchmarking Study. https://papers.ssrn.com/sol3/papers.cfm?abstract_id=3040224. Accessed 24 March 2018.

Holmes, C. 2017. Distributed Ledger Technologies for Public Good: Leadership, Collaboration and Innovation. http://chrisholmes.co.uk/wp-content/uploads/2017/11/Distributed-Ledger-Technologies-for-Public-Good_leadership-collaboration-and-innovation.pdf. Accessed 2 March 2018.

Howkins, J. 2007. *The Creative Economy*, updated edition. London: Penguin.

IFPI. 2017. Global Music Report 2017. http://www.ifpi.org/downloads/GMR2017.pdf. Accessed 10 November 2017.

Kranzberg, M. 1995. Technology and History: 'Kranzberg's Laws'. *Bulletin of Science, Technology & Society* 15 (1): 5–13.

Lessig, L. 2006. *Code Version 2.0*. New York: Basic Books.

Lundy, L., J. John, H. McLaverty, and S. Noor. 2018. The Convergence Ecosystem: Convergence 2.0—Building the Decentralised Future. https://outlierventures.io/wp-content/uploads/2018/03/The_Convergence_Ecosystem_Report_Outlier_Ventures_2018.pdf. Accessed 1 July 2018.

McAfee, A., and E. Brynjolfsson. 2017. *Machine Platform Crowd: Harnessing Our Digital Future*. New York and London: Norton.

Monetary Authority Singapore. 2017. A Guide to Digital Token Offerings. http://www.mas.gov.sg/~/media/MAS/Regulations%20and%20Financial%20Stability/Regulations%20Guidance%20and%20Licensing/Securities%20Futures%20and%20Fund%20Management/Regulations%20Guidance%20and%20Licensing/Guidelines/A%20Guide%20to%20Digital%20Token%20Offerings%20%2014%20Nov%202017.pdf. Accessed 1 July 2018.

Nakamoto, S. 2008. Bitcoin: A Peer-to-Peer Electronic Cash System. https://bitcoin.org/bitcoin.pdf. Accessed 24 March 2018.

Schwab, K. 2016. *The Fourth Industrial Revolution*. London: Portfolio Penguin.

Tapscott, D., and A. Tapscott. 2017. *Realising the Potential of Blockchain: A Multistakeholder Approach to the Stewardship of Blockchain and Cryptocurrencies*. World Economic Forum. http://www3.weforum.org/docs/WEF_Realizing_Potential_Blockchain.pdf. Accessed 10 November 2017.

Tapscott, D., and A. Tapscott. 2018. *Blockchain Revolution: How the Technology Behind Bitcoin and Other Cryptocurrencies is Changing the World*, updated edition. New York: Penguin Random House.

Taylor, S. 2017. https://11fs.com/blog/open-source-token-best-practice/. Accessed 3 July 2018.

Tucker, C., and C. Catalini. 2018. What Blockchain Can't Do. *Harvard Business Review*. https://hbr.org/2018/06/what-blockchain-cant-do. Accessed 29 June 2018.

Walport, M. (ed.). 2016. *Distributed Ledger Technology: Beyond Blockchain*. London: Wordlink. www.gov.uk/government/uploads/system/uploads/attachment_data/file/492972/gs-16-1-distributed-ledger-technology.pdf. Accessed 3 February 2016.

Young, S., and E. Cauldwell-French. 2018. The True Value of Creative Industries Digital Exports. Creative Industries Federation. https://www.creativeindustriesfederation.com/sites/default/files/2018-03/Federation%20Cebr%20CIC%20The%20true%20value%20of%20creative%20industries%20digital%20exports.pdf. Accessed 2 May 2018.

CHAPTER 7

Interview Transcripts

Abstract This chapter comprises transcripts of structured interviews with representatives of 10 creative economy start-ups working with blockchain technology. These interviews were conducted, via email, in May and early June 2018. The respondents were selected as representative of a range of different creative industries, and as at least relatively advanced in their adoption of the technology. Some of these responses are quoted elsewhere in the book. They are included here in full in order to show that the arguments put forward in the rest of the book are based on critical analysis of all available data, rather than carefully selected extracts. The interviews are also intended to serve as case studies, illustrating some of the many possible applications of blockchain technology within the creative economy.

Keywords Blockchain case studies · Blockchain interviews
Blockchain use cases

M. O'Dair, *Distributed Creativity*,
https://doi.org/10.1007/978-3-030-00190-2_7

Company: Artos

Interview respondent: Andy Grant (Chief Technology Officer)

Introduction
Please state the name of your business, its location(s), and the year in which it was launched.

Aventus Protocol Foundation, JTC House, 28 Esplanade, St Helier, Jersey, 2017.

Artos Systems Ltd, Office 502, 160 Fleet Street, London, 2018.

What problem is your business attempting to solve?

The Aventus Protocol has been developed to revolutionise the ticketing industry by giving ticketing rights holders greater control and security over inventory pricing and transactions. This will virtually eliminate ticketing fraud and unregulated, unethical touting activities.

How developed is your use case (e.g. minimum viable product, proof of concept etc.*)?*

The alpha version of the Aventus Protocol was released in July 2017. The first version of the source code (minimum viable product) was released in April 2018, and the Protocol is now in beta on the ethereum mainnet.

Which blockchain are you using and how are you using it (i.e. what is in the blocks and what is off-chain, public or private)?

The Aventus Protocol is an open standard built upon the ethereum network. Ticketing inventory is released onto the blockchain with an associated set of rules, selected by the inventory holder (such as minimum and maximum price caps). No user data is held upon the blockchain; this is retained off-chain.

Business Model and Value System
How important is blockchain technology to your business model and why? Please consider value proposition; market; operations; and finances:

- *Value proposition (i.e. the reason a specific group of customers come to you rather than a competitor)*:
  The Aventus Protocol Foundation is a non-profit entity dedicated to promoting innovation in the ticketing industry through the Aventus Protocol, which is an open source project created for the

good of the ticketing industry as a whole. As an organisation, openness and transparency lie at the heart of everything we do. Our primary commercial partner, Artos Systems Ltd, has been envisaged as a professional services layer being run on top of the open source project to partner with ticketing providers in order to develop consumer-facing ticketing apps and services.

- *Market (i.e. your customers, your relationships with those customers, and your channels for reaching those customers, before, during and after a sale)*:
  Due to being fully funded, we can afford to take a more long-term strategic view. This gives us the opportunity to build longer-term relationships with other parties in the industry, and focus on working with them to drive real business change.
- *Operations (i.e. your human, intellectual, financial and physical resources, your day-to-day activities, and your partnerships)*:
  Being involved in a cutting-edge, challenging technology with an open source flavour means that it's easier to attract top quality developers who want to work on something new and interesting.
- *Finances (i.e. your revenue streams and cost structure)*:
  The Aventus Protocol Foundation issued AVT and indirectly sold it for 60,000 ETH. This is strategically being deployed to further the Aventus protocol and associated ecosystem through various third parties.

How important is blockchain technology to your value system (i.e. the value chain as it extends beyond your specific company to suppliers, distributors and customers) and why?

The nature of the public blockchain means that as well as acting as a data layer, the protocol also acts as a communications layer. Anyone who understands its properties can build apps and services upon it: it's an open-source platform that allows anyone to build powerful decentralised applications for the ticketing industry.

Opportunities, Barriers, Risks

What do you consider the main benefits that blockchain technology can offer, both to your business and across your industry more broadly?

For ticketing agencies and ticketing software providers, the blockchain can provide a secure, immutable ledger of ticketing transactions between all parties in the ticketing ecosystem: primary sellers, secondary sellers, venues, promoters and fans. The true advantage of the blockchain is the level of control it brings to rights holders, who can set parameters around how, when and who by their tickets are resold—delivering palpable business benefits such as better consumer experience, reputational advantages associated with fairer pricing, and new revenue streams as a % of secondary market sales.

What do you consider the main barriers to adoption, both within your company and beyond, and how might those barriers be overcome? Please consider political, economic, social, technological, legal and/or environmental factors.

At the moment, the main barrier to adoption is the uncertain regulatory environment. It always takes a while for legal frameworks to catch up with any new technology, and even longer until any worldwide consensus is reached—at the moment, we're looking at a very fragmented global landscape. There are also legitimate environmental concerns around the energy required to support a blockchain. We believe these are short-term; work being done at the moment around Proof of Stake will ultimately alleviate the issue. There's a lot of education required, both in the industry and in society as a whole; we're actively working to provide that education piece, through the media and through things such industry roundtables, speaking on conference panels, and generally doing all we can to engage both with the ticketing and events world and across all markets.

What do you consider the risks—to your company and beyond—of adopting blockchain technology? Again, please consider political, economic, social, technological, legal and/or environmental factors.

The maximum capacity of the ethereum network is about 20 transactions per second: in computing terms, this sort of speed was surpassed back in the 1950s. There are several active projects in the ethereum community which are seeking to address this but for now speed is a challenge. In our view, though, technology choices are always about trade-offs. If you want something fast, there's a cost; in this case, we're prioritising security, transparency and control over speed.

Final Questions

What do you see as the likely timeline, both for your company and for the broader adoption of blockchain technology?

We've got several proof-of-concept partnerships taking place this year, across the worlds of music, sports and entertainment. Our commercial partner Artos Systems Ltd has been specifically developed as a professional services offering in order to help drive blockchain adoption within the ticketing industry itself. By partnering with ticketing organisations looking to get the business benefits from the Aventus Protocol, we can work with them to create user-facing apps and solutions. This is where consumers and ticketing organisers will start to really get value from this new technology; after all, even the most innovative technology isn't worth much if it can't actually be used. More broadly, timelines are difficult to predict with any degree of certainty. A lot of that is to do with the regulatory landscape, which desperately needs clarification. We'd estimate that mass adoption will come about five years following regulatory clarity.

What is the biggest misconception about adopting blockchain technology within the creative industries?

As far as the layperson is concerned, there are a lot of misconceptions around blockchain—particularly around the volatility of cryptocurrencies, given that bitcoin is the most well-known use-case and is often conflated with the blockchain as a whole. There's a popular conception that blockchain is a buzzword and a bubble and people are just out to make a quick buck. Within the technical community itself, some blockchain advocates haven't fully considered the complexities of the problem they're trying to solve, which will ultimately affect the efficacy of solutions and their adoption.

What one step could policy-makers take to promote the adoption of blockchain technology in the creative industries in what you would consider a positive manner?

There's a while to go before the legal framework catches up with any new technology, and longer to go before any worldwide consensus is reached. At the moment, we're looking at a very fragmented legal landscape. We would welcome clarity in this area: if you don't know the rules it's hard to play the game! A worldwide consortium devoted to engaging with governments around the world, educating consumers, lobbying for adoption and demystifying the technology would be a good positive step to bringing about that clarity.

Company: Blokur

Interview respondent: Phil Barry (Founder)

Introduction
Please state the name of your business, its location(s), and the year in which it was launched.

Blokur. London and Oxford. 2016.

What problem is your business attempting to solve?
Inaccuracy and inefficiency in music rights attribution.

How developed is your use case (e.g. minimum viable product, proof of concept etc.*)?*
Live Beta.

Which blockchain are you using and how are you using it (i.e. what is in the blocks and what is off-chain, public or private)?
Public ethereum blockchain. Abstractions of music rights and usage information are written to the blockchain.

Business Model and Value System
How important is blockchain technology to your business model and why? Please consider value proposition; market; operations; and finances:

- *Value proposition (i.e. the reason a specific group of customers come to you rather than a competitor)*:
  Blockchain is an important part of the value proposition in (1) presenting an alternative to centralised approaches which have generally failed due to governance and ownership problems solved by blockchain technology and (2) providing an auditable audit trail of music rights ownership and usage over time.
- *Market (i.e. your customers, your relationships with those customers, and your channels for reaching those customers, before, during and after a sale)*:
  Blokur's interactions with customers are broadly similar to any enterprise software company. The go-to-market model is defined at the application layer, which in Blokur's case is SAAS [Software as a Service].
- *Operations (i.e. your human, intellectual, financial and physical resources, your day-to-day activities, and your partnerships)*:
  While building applications on ethereum does require specific capabilities in terms of software engineering, Blokur has generally focused on developing these through training rather than hiring experienced blockchain expertise. At this early stage in the ecosystem, overfocusing on blockchain experience does not necessarily ensure that you are attracting the most able candidates. Using ethereum creates a dependency upon an open software community. But Blokur considers this a more attractive option than building

out and owning its own blockchain infrastructure since by definition networks benefit from having multiple participants, and the ethereum community is able to release updates at a much faster rate than could be achieved by a single company. Blokur has also built some of its own technology that will ultimately be released open source because it contributes to the scalability of the ecosystem as whole, which is important both to Blokur and the wider community.

- *Finances (i.e. your revenue streams and cost structure)*:
  There is a small variable cost of reading and writing data to and from the blockchain, which is a very small proportion of the overall cost structure.

How important is blockchain technology to your value system (i.e. the value chain as it extends beyond your specific company to suppliers, distributors and customers) and why?

Blockchain is important to the connectivity of the value chain because it provides an efficient interaction model for a group of diverse participants. A function of Blokur's decision to use blockchain technology, therefore, is that the rights value chain looks much more like an ecosystem and less like a linear value chain in terms of data flow.

Opportunities, Barriers, Risks

What do you consider the main benefits that blockchain technology can offer, both to your business and across your industry more broadly?

The opportunity for Blokur is to use blockchain technology to underpin a new model for multi-party interactions that solves our customers' data problems. More broadly, blockchain technology is a shared infrastructure that allows data and automation to live outside of a traditional corporate structure, which represents a big leap forward in terms of efficiency and co-ordination.

What do you consider the main barriers to adoption, both within your company and beyond, and how might those barriers be overcome? Please consider political, economic, social, technological, legal and/or environmental factors.

[No answer on the record]

What do you consider the risks—to your company and beyond—of adopting blockchain technology? Again, please consider political, economic, social, technological, legal and/or environmental factors.

Today's blockchains have well-reported limitations of scale and cost-efficiency that will need to be overcome. Therefore, there is some risk in the need to rely on future upgrades and improvements. But history suggests that, while it's difficult to predict which implementation is going to be the most successful, the market will drive the necessary innovation to bring the technology to maturity. In the meantime, it's necessary to build applications in a modular way to reduce dependency on any one blockchain technology.

Final Questions
What do you see as the likely timeline, both for your company and for the broader adoption of blockchain technology?

I would expect to see significant mainstream adoption over the next twelve months.

What is the biggest misconception about adopting blockchain technology within the creative industries?

Because blockchain is still a relatively new technology, very few user-facing products and services exist. As a result, people spend a lot of time talking about the underlying technology itself, rather than the thing that people and businesses will interact with. This sometimes has the effect of making it seem that blockchain technology will be difficult to adopt from a technology and systems perspective. In fact, it is perfectly possible that in many cases people will use an application that leverages blockchain technology without knowing that a blockchain is even being used.

What one step could policy-makers take to promote the adoption of blockchain technology in the creative industries in what you would consider a positive manner?

The single most helpful thing UK policy-makers could do would be to guarantee the UK's future membership of the European single market and European copyright framework.

Company: Civil

Interview respondent: Christine Mohan (Co-founder)

Introduction
Please state the name of your business, its location(s), and the year in which it was launched.

Civil is headquartered in Brooklyn, NY with a global team located in San Francisco, Boston, Washington DC and Warsaw, Poland. Civil formed in 2017.

What problem is your business attempting to solve?

We're aiming to support sustainable journalism throughout the world. The ad-driven revenue model that traditionally funded quality journalism has not translated to the digital economy. Civil is committed to introducing a new funding model using blockchain and cryptoeconomics that enables journalists to focus on reporting, rather than satisfying clicks-over-quality mandates from third parties like advertisers and publishers.

How developed is your use case (e.g. minimum viable product, proof of concept etc.*)?*

Our initial publishing platform or MVP [Minimum Viable Product] launches in June 2018 with 13+ newsrooms. The Civil Registry, which will launch this summer, will mark the point at which any interested party can apply to launch a Newsroom on Civil.

Which blockchain are you using and how are you using it (i.e. what is in the blocks and what is off-chain, public or private)?

We are using the ethereum blockchain. Some of the newsroom content will be stored off-chain on our content management system to ensure low latency (e.g., to ensure pages load quickly!). The content management system will allow Newsrooms to upload articles directly to the ethereum blockchain's distributed, public ledger, making them nearly impossible to delete without co-opting an independent network of hundreds of thousands of computers. Future token use cases will also be applied to both licensing and membership models, among other utilities.

Business Model and Value System

Our revenue model is focused on fostering an active ecosystem of apps and services, similar to an App Store economy. The Civil Media Company does not take a cut of the revenue between journalists and readers. We will take a small portion of the transactions from tools created by developers for our ecosystem. And we will announce a token sale in June 2018 that will help fund the growth, adoption and evolution of the Civil protocol.

In terms of value system, we will be announcing the Civil Foundation dedicated to supporting vital journalism efforts around Civil's core values of open and inclusive reporting and press freedoms. We've also announced Civil Studios, a journalism-focused venture-builder for the decentralised web, which will be a for-profit venture. Civil Studios will work on projects at the intersection of blockchain and media, and will be a laboratory for promoting sustainability and profitability in journalism. These initiatives will strengthen the core Civil news platform while driving new readers, journalists and partners into the ecosystem.

How important is blockchain technology to your business model and why? Please consider value proposition; market; operations; and finances:

Blockchain technology is critical to our business model of creating a decentralised platform for sustainable journalism. Blockchain enables self-governance (CVL tokens represent ownership in a cooperative network, and also act as voting chips for the community governance model) and permanence (permanent recording of authorship and content, via the blockchain's distributed ledger). The Civil Registry is what makes Civil truly different from other journalism models; we're introducing cryptoeconomic incentives, underpinned by the Civil Constitution, a foundational, 'rules of the road' document for behaviour on Civil, to ensure that rational behaviour scales with the network, and that special interests aren't able to co-opt the platform's governance model. Inclusion in the Civil Registry means that the community has vetted a Newsroom and deemed it as having a credible, journalistic mission. A Newsroom's status on the Civil Registry can be challenged at any time, if it's found to be in serious violation of the Civil Constitution.

- *Value proposition (i.e. the reason a specific group of customers come to you rather than a competitor)*:
  We have three main customer bases and value propositions: Newsmakers will come to us for the opportunity to run a newsroom independently; our blockchain model also strengthens protections for journalists against censorship and intellectual property violations. Readers will come to read exclusive, vetted content and support newsrooms directly with no middleman (publisher, owner, advertiser). Finally, developers will be able to build, market and sell their applications on Civil, the first blockchain journalism platform.
- *Market (i.e. your customers, your relationships with those customers, and your channels for reaching those customers, before, during and after a sale)*:
  At first Civil will be a two-sided marketplace of journalists (Newsmakers) and readers (Citizens). Eventually we may add advertisers to our marketplace. For marketing channels before launch,

we've built a strong base of followers across our email newsletter and social media including organic and paid campaign growth; we've also secured comprehensive press coverage about Civil's model. During our news platform and token sale launches, we will focus on proactive, daily management of Telegram and Twitter to respond to questions and foster adoption and usage. After launch, we will continue to promote Civil to prospective newsrooms and drive readership across the platform. We will also continue to host Civil meet-ups and speak at journalism and blockchain events worldwide. Finally, in terms of widespread adoption, readers will be able to support Civil however they choose; cryptocurrency is NOT a barrier to entry on Civil.

- *Operations (i.e. your human, intellectual, financial and physical resources, your day-to-day activities, and your partnerships)*:
  Civil current has 22 employees in five locations worldwide. We are a 'spoke' of ConsenSys, the largest ethereum venture studio, and collaborate closely with other ConsenSys spokes or blockchain projects to leverage their tools and expertise including Alethio (an ethereum analytics platform), Metamask (an ethereum DApp browser), and Token Foundry (a token distribution platform).
- *Finances (i.e. your revenue streams and cost structure)*:
  Civil Newsrooms will independently determine and manage their revenue streams (membership, paid content tiers, microtipping). The Civil Media Company will derive revenue from Civil Studios, our token launch, and from a portion of marketplace transactions. Our cost structure is the tech stack necessary for our platform and token model; as well as the operational costs of Civil Studios, Civil Labs and the Civil Foundation. Newsrooms will manage their own costs (staffing, marketing, design).

How important is blockchain technology to your value system (i.e. the value chain as it extends beyond your specific company to suppliers, distributors and customers) and why?

Please see above.

Opportunities, Barriers, Risks

Consumer adoption, especially mainstream consumers, is both an opportunity and a risk. Civil aims to be the first consumer-facing application on the blockchain, due to our news model and mainstream audience. Barriers to entry include the volatility of cryptocurrency and exaggerated news headlines, which may create wariness in non-financial, non-technical consumers who see cryptocurrency investment as risky.

What do you consider the main benefits that blockchain technology can offer, both to your business and across your industry more broadly?

The immediate benefits to Civil include governance for community management and quality control; permanence through blockchain's immutable archive as a censorship-resistant tool; privacy or 'pseudonymity' as a protection for journalists; and decentralisation to create independent newsrooms. Established corporations in the creative industry currently dictate the relationship and revenue exchange between creator and consumer. Blockchain technology can help level this playing field. Companies like Ujo, SingularDTV and Cellarius are utilising blockchain to disrupt the current, centralised media business models in music, broadcast and publishing. Restoring ownership rights to the creators, creating more efficient and frictionless payment models, protecting copyrights, and enabling peer-to-peer distribution are critical to autonomy.

What do you consider the main barriers to adoption, both within your company and beyond, and how might those barriers be overcome? Please consider political, economic, social, technological, legal and/or environmental factors.

The peer-to-peer nature of blockchain technology, where content creators can transact directly and immediately with content consumers—without middlemen—has implications for all creative industries: journalism and media, entertainment, film, music. Established players will inevitably create barriers to prevent these connections; creatives and consumers need to continue to push the boundaries and status quo.

What do you consider the risks—to your company and beyond—of adopting blockchain technology? Again, please consider political, economic, social, technological, legal and/or environmental factors.

News consumers and media companies are core users and partners for Civil, yet few mainstream consumers understand blockchain or cryptocurrency. We need to offer exclusive, high-quality news experiences and drive usage from casual readers to community governance through token ownership. Beyond Civil, global media firms are currently investigating blockchain options and platforms, but may not be ready (strategically, psychologically or financially) to commit to such a nascent technology. Instead they may prefer to focus on emergent technologies (AR, VR, AI, machine learning) or continue to innovate within more familiar technologies (video, podcasts, mobile).

Final Questions

What do you see as the likely timeline, both for your company and for the broader adoption of blockchain technology?

Civil plans to launch 1000 newsrooms globally over the next 1–2 years. We're simultaneously building a robust marketplace for developers and the larger news ecosystem (photographers, videographers, graphic designers), to offer services and tools for these newsrooms. In the coming year, we'll also partner with top media and technology firms to offer syndication, archiving, discourse, polling, identity, licensing and curation services to expand the reach of our newsrooms.

What is the biggest misconception about adopting blockchain technology within the creative industries?

Some creative firms may feel that it's too early to investigate and adopt blockchain technology; that the technology is untested, not relevant; or that the consumer is not ready. Those who take a 'wait and see' approach will miss out on early industry developments and learnings. The time to experiment and build blockchain expertise is now.

What one step could policy-makers take to promote the adoption of blockchain technology in the creative industries in what you would consider a positive manner?

Policy-makers could support the training of high school and community college students, across diverse backgrounds, to learn the programming languages needed for blockchain, smart contracts and cryptocurrency. Blockchain engineers are already in high demand; the pay is higher than many other software engineer roles, and a talented engineer can work from anywhere in the world. Today's journalism schools train students how to code; tomorrow's liberal arts programs need to train students in blockchain technologies.

Company: CryptoKitties

Interview respondent: Bryce Bladon (Founding Team Member)

Introduction

Please state the name of your business, its location(s), and the year in which it was launched.

CryptoKitties. Vancouver, Canada. 2017.

What problem is your business attempting to solve?

- Show a consumer case for blockchain technology
- Showcase a non-cryptocurrency application for blockchain technology
- Dispel myths and help educate the world on the wider implications of blockchain technology.

How developed is your use case (e.g. minimum viable product, proof of concept etc.*)?*

We're less than a year old, with $24 m++ in transactions and hundreds of thousands of users. We launched a practical product from day one.

Which blockchain are you using and how are you using it (i.e. what is in the blocks and what is off-chain, public or private)?

Ethereum. All breeding, collection, and storage is hosted on the blockchain. We host our marketplace on a centralised site, but the actual transactions—all the decentralised features of blockchain—utilise the blockchain network.

Business Model and Value System

How important is blockchain technology to your business model and why? Please consider value proposition; market; operations; and finances:

It's fundamental; our vision is to bring the first billion people to the blockchain.

- *Value proposition (i.e. the reason a specific group of customers come to you rather than a competitor)*:
  We are the world's most successful blockchain-based game and a cultural sensation covered by the BBC, the NYT, VICE, and numerous other publications. We pioneered the now-standard non-fungible token, ERC-721, which has numerous implications for a variety of creative applications of blockchain technology.
- *Market (i.e. your customers, your relationships with those customers, and your channels for reaching those customers, before, during and after a sale)*:
  Our player base is a mix of blockchain enthusiasts and consumers who were looking for an accessible introduction to the technology. Outside of an excellent user experience, we primarily focus on community-building tools: we have an active Discord, newsletter, Twitter, etc.

- *Operations (i.e. your human, intellectual, financial and physical resources, your day-to-day activities, and your partnerships)*:
  We are a team of designers, developers, engineers, and dreamers from a diverse range of backgrounds. Originally created by Axiom Zen, we received $12 M+ from Andreessen Horowitz, Union Square Ventures, and a variety of other remarkable investors. Following that, we formed a formal and independent company.
- *Finances (i.e. your revenue streams and cost structure)*:
  Outside of partnerships and special auctions, we make 3.75% of each sale conducted on our marketplace and 100% of the proceeds of 'Gen 0' cats, which are released every fifteen minutes for the first year of our product's life.

How important is blockchain technology to your value system (i.e. the value chain as it extends beyond your specific company to suppliers, distributors and customers) and why?

It's crucial, though we do solve some UX [user experience] challenges with centralised solutions to provide the best possible consumer experience.

Opportunities, Barriers, Risks

What do you consider the main benefits that blockchain technology can offer, both to your business and across your industry more broadly?

Blockchain offers numerous benefits to consumers and creators alike. With the understanding that blockchain's main use case is to allow two parties to trade value with no one in the middle, it also allows that value to take many new forms. This unlocks numerous benefits: true ownership, provenance, accessibility (no, really), decentralised economics, proof of provenance, transparent transactions, democratised investment, and digital art sales through digital scarcity.

What do you consider the main barriers to adoption, both within your company and beyond, and how might those barriers be overcome? Please consider political, economic, social, technological, legal and/or environmental factors.

Simply put, centralised solutions are more convenient: they're familiar, they're faster, and they're entrenched. Blockchain technology still has substantial barriers to overcome in the form of obsoletion, speculation and stability, computation, and scalability. That last one is the big one.

What do you consider the risks—to your company and beyond—of adopting blockchain technology? Again, please consider political, economic, social, technological, legal and/or environmental factors.

A combination of excitement and ignorance is a dangerous thing. Bad players and scam artists are often found at that junction as well. If blockchain technology manages to become ubiquitous, the environmental impact needs to be mitigated.

Final Questions

What do you see as the likely timeline, both for your company and for the broader adoption of blockchain technology?

It's going to be at least a few years before the blockchain technology sees widespread adoption. However, numerous niche applications are already proving viable and a variety of large-scale projects should come to fruition in the interim. Their impact will reduce or increase the overall timeline.

What is the biggest misconception about adopting blockchain technology within the creative industries?

The biggest misconception I see is that it is only a technology for engineers, financiers, and Silicon Valley enthusiasts. Blockchain holds immense creative potential, especially in the formal art industry.

What one step could policy-makers take to promote the adoption of blockchain technology in the creative industries in what you would consider a positive manner?

CryptoKitties worked with local regulators prior to launching. Though it was time-consuming, it was a process that benefitted both parties and ensured the best possible scenario for consumers. Be proactive and make education a central feature for all parties involved.

Company: FilmChain

Interview respondents: Irina Albita (Co-founder), Jamie Sly (Community and Content) and Maria Tanjala (Co-founder)

Introduction

Please state the name of your business, its location(s), and the year in which it was launched.

Big Couch is HQd in London since 2014. In 2017, Big Couch launched FilmChain.

What problem is your business attempting to solve?

Once a film is produced, it goes on the film market for sale. Every exhibitor of a film (cinemas, VOD [Video On Demand] platforms, broadcasters, etc.) becomes a revenue collection source. Outside the studio system, only a few companies service the entire film market, creating issues for the independent film industry which is plagued by three main problems:

- Accessibility: independent films entering the market are unable to afford the high service fees with their lower budgets, resulting in up to 70% of independent films going uncatered for.
- Transparency: little access to real-time information. The stakeholders, or even the film producers, have no authority, no traceability and, often, no auditing power.
- Complexity: coordinating projects and stakeholders in contractual agreements is a manual, and lengthy, process. This delays payments and creates friction between film stakeholders.

How developed is your use case (e.g. minimum viable product, proof of concept etc.*)?*

Big Couch is a fully operating platform and has co-financed films alongside some of the biggest organisations in the UK and Europe, including the British Film Institute, Creative Scotland, Icelandic Film Centre, Marina Abramovic Institute. FilmChain is in its Alpha stage, with three major film projects signed up to test out the platform starting August 2018.

Which blockchain are you using and how are you using it (i.e. what is in the blocks and what is off-chain, public or private)?

FilmChain is a platform for revenue collection and allocation and utilises the ethereum blockchain. FilmChain uses ethereum blockchain in order to increase transparency in the film and digital industries, utilising smart contracts to cut down on settlement times and decrease costs for everyone invested: financiers, equity investors, producers, crews, cast, etc. The prototype focuses on the optimisation of business processes and allows independent filmmakers access revenues instantly. When new revenue appears, a proprietary network of smart contracts automatically allocates tokens based on our algorithm, removing the need for a middleman. Stakeholders log onto their dashboards and can withdraw the amounts in their wallets, paid in fiat. The use of blockchain also allows a fully transparent ledger of transactions for the producers, who can verify the incomes of their projects. The platform has different layers of privacy that enables each stakeholder to track their own income streams. The dashboards also provide revenue analyses to empower producers to make informed decisions over marketing spent, for future investment decisions, audiences tracking etc.

Business Model and Value System
How important is blockchain technology to your business model and why? Please consider value proposition; market; operations; and finances.

- *Value proposition (i.e. the reason a specific group of customers come to you rather than a competitor)*:
  Blockchain allows for the transparency of transactions, empowering filmmakers and crewmembers, as they will know exactly where their money is. The users also benefit from increased share of revenue whilst drastically reducing overheads and cutting down middlemen. This is achieved by minimising time and resource wastage, with a greater focus on transparency and productivity. It is open to any budget, collects revenues globally and processes nanopayments instantly. Furthermore, we take away the legal hassle surrounding contracts, putting in place a transparent and unbiased legal framework, allowing creatives to focus on creating their dream vision without worrying about the admin. Finally, we analyse sources of revenues and implement rights management tracker.
- *Market (i.e. your customers, your relationships with those customers, and your channels for reaching those customers, before, during and after a sale)*:
  The channels of communication stay the same, film festival markets, industry publications, social media, word-of-mouth etc. We do not want to massively change behaviours for our customers, so we are somewhat hiding the complexity of the technology, while building user friendly and accessible interfaces. We want any producer, investor, financier, crew, actor, with any level of tech knowledge, to be able to use our platform.
- *Operations (i.e. your human, intellectual, financial and physical resources, your day-to-day activities, and your partnerships)*:
  In terms of operations, blockchain allows the automation of roles that would have previously taken individuals time to manually

integrate and execute. This automation provided by blockchain allows the optimisation of business processes, enabling people to devote their time to the areas that matter, freeing up time from unnecessary workloads. We are consolidating partnerships with blockchain platforms and members of the ecosystem. We are in close communication with ConsenSys (ethereum) and we are part of EU Blockchain Observatory & Forum. It is key to keep updated on the latest developments, tools and regulations.

- *Finances (i.e. your revenue streams and cost structure)*:
  Blockchain is vital to the financial structure of the FilmChain platform as it manages the collection and allocation of revenues arising from specific projects, all autonomously. This significantly lowers prices in several areas of operations.

How important is blockchain technology to your value system (i.e. the value chain as it extends beyond your specific company to suppliers, distributors and customers) and why?

The film value chain is determined by several stages: financing, development, production, post-production, sale, distribution and exhibition. Throughout all these stages, a new business model, powered by blockchain technology, is making a strong move. Integrated solutions from financing to exhibition are taking shape. The encompassing vision for blockchain solutions is to enable, at the point of the content consumption, a real-time allocation of revenues with anyone that has worked on a project. Our only reservation at the moment is around the financing stage—where, in an unclear regulatory landscape, financing films though Initial Token/Coin Offerings is not yet a viable solution. Currently, FilmChain is taking a realistic step-by-step development approach, working within the boundaries of the current film business model to present a real alternative to collection services and real-time monitoring of revenues.

Opportunities, Barriers, Risks

What do you consider the main benefits that blockchain technology can offer, both to your business and across your industry more broadly?

Blockchain technology is a game changer when it comes to the screen industry. Smart contracts have the potential to disrupt various roles within the sector as they allow agreements to be automatically validated, signed and executed by utilising the blockchain ledger. This is important because it removes the need for a middleman and the high fees they charge. Blockchain technology is also useful due to the transparency of the system, allowing individuals to track incoming revenues and how the money was split amongst film stakeholders or digital content creators. Blockchain is useful in tracking ownership, recording digital assets and avoiding ownership disputes.

What do you consider the main barriers to adoption, both within your company and beyond, and how might those barriers be overcome? Please consider political, economic, social, technological, legal and/or environmental factors.

- A major hurdle blockchain has to overcome is the accessibility of the platform. Many people are unaware of blockchains existence, and those who are, often struggle to comprehend the intricacies behind the technology.
- End users still have a strong preference for utilising fiat. Fiat-to-cryptocurrency exchanges are a developing market.
- The scalability of blockchain and processing huge amounts of transactions.
- The message that often comes associated with blockchain and the way the media portrays the new technology—words such as 'disintermediation' and 'speculation' are often circulated and do not put at ease many film stakeholders. At FilmChain, we believe it is very important to make a clear distinction between cryptocurrencies and the underlying value of the blockchain technology.

What do you consider the risks—to your company and beyond—of adopting blockchain technology? Again, please consider political, economic, social, technological, legal and/or environmental factors.

Some of the main risks that come with the adoption of blockchain technology for our company and others are the potential regulatory and legal restrictions that could be put in place. There are also issues surrounding settlements and if the blockchain ledger is evidence of ownership from a legal and regulatory perspective. Technologically, while we are developing as protocol-agnostic as possible, we do have a massive buy-in into the ethereum platform—the blockchain protocol with the largest support communities. The way this protocol will develop and the strength of its governance systems are very important for us.

Final Questions

What do you see as the likely timeline, both for your company and for the broader adoption of blockchain technology?

During the summer of 2018, FilmChain is running an Alpha product. We aim to have a Beta version of our platform by the beginning of 2019. The broader adoption of the technology is dependant on the issues surrounding scalability and if more people decide to actively get engaged with the technology. There is currently a shortage of technical and non-technical professionals who are experts in building reliable applications and [who can] help the ecosystem grow.

What is the biggest misconception about adopting blockchain technology within the creative industries?

Many creators are excited about the implications blockchain has for the creative industries due to the increased control it gives them over their work and rights. Yet, despite this, there are still very few real-life applications of blockchain, as many people believe that the technology is costly and difficult to implement. This is untrue, as the underlying technology is free for anybody to use, something which many people are unaware of. Another popular misconception of blockchain is that people believe blockchain = bitcoin. This is troublesome as they associate the legal issues surrounding bitcoin with blockchain and fail to understand how the technology can be utilised outside of speculative nature of cryptocurrencies.

What one step could policy-makers take to promote the adoption of blockchain technology in the creative industries in what you would consider a positive manner?

Governments should actively try to promote Blockchain technology by:

- Providing more R&D funding for tech companies to explore the benefits.
- Drafting a clear regulatory framework to govern the launch and growth of blockchain-driven initiatives.
- Supporting more education around the space by commissioning industry papers, organising trade working groups and collaborating with universities.

Company: GUTS

Interview respondent: Olivier Biggs (Communication and Community Management)

Introduction
Please state the name of your business, its location(s), and the year in which it was launched.

GUTS tickets. We are in Amsterdam, the Netherlands, and have been around since late 2015.

What problem is your business attempting to solve?

We are putting an end to ticket fraud and ticket touting by merging the first and secondary markets, using blockchain technology. We have done so by developing the 'GET protocol', which creates smart tickets that prevents fraud and scalping.

How developed is your use case (e.g. minimum viable product, proof of concept etc.)?

We are fully operational and have been for quite some time. As of this writing (June 2018), we have already sold over 50,000 smart tickets this year, with signed partnerships that guarantee the sale of more than one million tickets in 2019.

Which blockchain are you using and how are you using it (i.e. what is in the blocks and what is off-chain, public or private)?

We are currently running on the Kovan network, which we use to (anonymously) register ownership of tickets, and changes in ownership. The personalised registration is linked to the visitor's phone number, the registration of which is stored privately. We will be switching to the main ethereum network within a few months. For future scaling purposes, we are exploring other options, but for now ethereum it is.

Business Model and Value System
How important is blockchain technology to your business model and why? Please consider value proposition; market; operations; and finances:

- *Value proposition (i.e. the reason a specific group of customers come to you rather than a competitor)*:

A constantly growing number of artists, managers and venues are interested in working with us because they see that the GET protocol is a definitive solution to the problems of ticket touting and fraud. The blockchain component of this system is what makes it transparent, hence solidifying its credibility.

- *Market (i.e. your customers, your relationships with those customers, and your channels for reaching those customers, before, during and after a sale)*:

We have a hybrid system, meaning the end users (ticket buyers) will not have to deal with confusing blockchain technology or cryptocurrencies; they just want to have their tickets and enjoy the show. GET protocol runs in the background and is the engine for every transaction. This is what mass adoption looks like to us; disrupting the way things work without forcing anyone to make substantial changes to their lifestyle.

- *Operations (i.e. your human, intellectual, financial and physical resources, your day-to-day activities, and your partnerships)*:

We use blockchain as an infrastructure. This means that clients, partners and most employees should hardly notice which infrastructure is being used. Think of it like the internet: it just has to work.

- *Finances (i.e. your revenue streams and cost structure)*:
- The integration of blockchain technology into the event industry provides a lot more clarity about who makes money and why. Every transaction is now traceable and the value of a ticket is immutable from the moment it is issued. No third parties step in and take profits, restoring the so-called value chain, fairly rewarding and compensating those who actually bring something to the table.

How important is blockchain technology to your value system (i.e. the value chain as it extends beyond your specific company to suppliers, distributors and customers) and why?

It is a crucial part, as it finally provides transparency in the value chain, exposing the third parties that are now profiting from being able to act 'in the dark', so to speak. This allows them to, for example, easily buy up hundreds or thousands of tickets for a popular concert and sell these tickets back to fans for profit without having to account for their actions. An innovative application of blockchain technology sheds a light on this process and shows who is profiting and when, providing easier ways of restructuring the value chain so the right actors receive the fair rewards.

Opportunities, Barriers, Risks

What do you consider the main benefits that blockchain technology can offer, both to your business and across your industry more broadly?

Transparency. It means that transactions are now publicly traceable and all actors involved can be held accountable for their actions. In the case of ticketing this means that no more fraudulent or opportunistic third parties can wedge themselves in between an event organiser and an event attendee to hold the tickets hostage for profit.

What do you consider the main barriers to adoption, both within your company and beyond, and how might those barriers be overcome? Please consider political, economic, social, technological, legal and/or environmental factors.

The first barrier is scalability. We plan on selling millions of tickets, for events that often release large batches of their tickets simultaneously. This means large amounts of traffic and transactions, that all need to go flawlessly. For this reason, we are constantly doing stress tests for our systems, that grow in scale and intensity each time, and include more and more edge cases, to achieve 100% success rate.

What do you consider the risks—to your company and beyond—of adopting blockchain technology? Again, please consider political, economic, social, technological, legal and/or environmental factors.

Because the industry that we are disrupting is so massive and mainstream, providing a blockchain-based solution can cause somewhat of a startled reaction at first. This goes especially for older consumers who are afraid that they will be forced to use complicated technology they don't (want to) understand. As soon as we can get across that this is not the case, these worries evaporate.

Final Questions

What do you see as the likely timeline, both for your company and for the broader adoption of blockchain technology?

There is growth for both. More directly for GUTS, as we are onboarding more and more artists, managements and venues that are standing up against ticket fraud and scalping. The more successful use cases we can build, the more interest grows in our ticketing solution.

As far as the broader adoption of blockchain technology, I believe there will be a filtering of unnecessary applications first. Since the appeal to apply a form of blockchain technology to any type of business is now so large, it is currently being applied to any and all businesses.

What is the biggest misconception about adopting blockchain technology within the creative industries?

Probably the idea that it requires everyone to get their own bitcoin wallets and be able to understand the workings of it. As is the case with any technology or system, there will be experts on it, but no one should be expected to learn the underlying system of something they are already using. The right application of blockchain makes things easier and safer, not more complicated.

What one step could policy-makers take to promote the adoption of blockchain technology in the creative industries in what you would consider a positive manner?

I believe the sooner that policy-makers get involved in supporting and applying blockchain technology where it has obvious benefits, the better. Now is the time for differentiation between progress and empty promises. Policy-makers with the GUTS to get behind blockchain progress now will also automatically benefit by making themselves popular amongst a substantial global demographic.

Company: JAAK

Interview respondent: Daniel Fowler (Strategy and Operations)

Introduction

Please state the name of your business, its location(s), and the year in which it was launched.

JAAK is a London-based technology company. We've spent the last four years investigating the potential for blockchain-enabled solutions in the music and media industries.

What problem is your business attempting to solve?

Working with key industry stakeholders, we have identified two problems that we believe that blockchain infrastructure could provide solutions to: an aggregated view of copyright—*who owns what*, and scalable licensing solutions—*lowering the barriers to content.*

How developed is your use case (e.g. minimum viable product, proof of concept etc.*)?*

We are in the process of concluding our private pilot (proof of concept) and transitioning towards building a minimum viable product.

Which blockchain are you using and how are you using it (i.e. what is in the blocks and what is off-chain, public or private)?

We are building within the ethereum ecosystem, utilising ethereum for state consensus and Swarm for decentralised storage.

Business Model and Value System

How important is blockchain technology to your business model and why? Please consider value proposition; market; operations; and finances:

- *Value proposition (i.e. the reason a specific group of customers come to you rather than a competitor)*:
- *Market (i.e. your customers, your relationships with those customers, and your channels for reaching those customers, before, during and after a sale)*:
- *Operations (i.e. your human, intellectual, financial and physical resources, your day-to-day activities, and your partnerships)*:
- *Finances (i.e. your revenue streams and cost structure)*:

The success of our project is reliant on creating a system that moves from the current structure of disproportionate risk-reward and competitive pressures, and towards one that enables transparent value distribution and cooperative pressure. Thus, it's absolutely important that we build across technology that enables this: combining incentive mechanisms with open decentralised design to encourage collaboration.

How important is blockchain technology to your value system (i.e. the value chain as it extends beyond your specific company to suppliers, distributors and customers) and why?

Transparent value distribution and decentralised shared infrastructure will reduce the requirement for parallel non-differentiating investment, and incentivise effort and resource towards value-adding services. The result of this will be an industry that has reduced friction in licensing and paying creators, lowers barriers to entry for those that want to contribute to the industry, and offers greater opportunities for users to be able to access content.

Opportunities, Barriers, Risks

What do you consider the main benefits that blockchain technology can offer, both to your business and across your industry more broadly?

The media industries are underpinned by a complicated rights structure and siloed information. This negatively impacts stakeholders with high supply chain costs and missed revenue opportunities. The industry has converged on a solution in the form of a global view of rights. However, previous centralised attempts to create this have failed, primarily due to the requirement for centralised control and governance, upfront industry-wide consensus, and misaligned incentives. We believe that blockchains and a decentralised approach offer a potential remedy due to their ability to enable (1) a network of participants; (2) to collaboratively maintain a single dataset; and (3) without a central authority.

What do you consider the main barriers to adoption, both within your company and beyond, and how might those barriers be overcome? Please consider political, economic, social, technological, legal and/or environmental factors.

The complexity of legacy technology, process, and data is a challenge; however, value is also incredibly consolidated, and rights are by their nature very sticky. We are building global infrastructure—a comprehensive network. Thus, any solution that we design needs to work for all rights holders. Balancing these requirements has been insurmountable to date and will require incentive mechanisms that build cooperative pressure. We believe that the best approach to do this is through extensive engagement with, and listening to, the users for whom we are building the network. This enables us to align short-term commercial interests of individual stakeholders with the long-term goals of the industry.

What do you consider the risks—to your company and beyond—of adopting blockchain technology? Again, please consider political, economic, social, technological, legal and/or environmental factors.

Blockchain technology is nascent, and building decentralised infrastructure is difficult. Things will break, and so there is an increased emphasis on the requirement for redundancy and robust design. The overarching regulatory environment and crypto investment backdrop are evolving. This requires projects to invest in areas that might not be a typical priority for equivalent teams developing centralised technology.

Final Questions

What do you see as the likely timeline, both for your company and for the broader adoption of blockchain technology?

We are starting to see projects deploy MVPs [Minimum Viable Products] to the ethereum mainnet, which will ramp up in earnest over the next 12 months. This will allow for the battle testing of token models and incentive mechanisms and spark the development of token engineering as a discipline, prompting the next phase of blockchain technology development. Our roadmap sees us releasing our first commercial solutions within this timeframe, along with the planned release of the live KORD network.

What is the biggest misconception about adopting blockchain technology within the creative industries?

A considerable amount of our time has been spent dispelling the 'blockchain myths' that have evolved over the past couple of years. Namely: (1) blockchains don't automatically solve data conflicts; (2) public blockchains don't require all data within them to be fully visible; and (3) perfect or minimum data is not a prerequisite—you cannot change history in a blockchain, but you can update information.

What one step could policy-makers take to promote the adoption of blockchain technology in the creative industries in what you would consider a positive manner?

The largest challenge facing blockchain projects at the moment is probably access to talent. The space is new and required skill sets consolidated to the few early adopters, thus demand is outstripping supply. Government-subsidised training and education schemes could have a considerable positive effect towards development. The space is primarily open source and community-driven. Therefore, there is the opportunity for governments to seize on the potential for making their country attractive as a centre for blockchain development through tax credits or other such financial incentives.

Company: Maecenas Fine Art

Interview respondent: Marcelo Garcia Casil (CEO)

Introduction

Please state the name of your business, its location(s), and the year in which it was launched.

Maecenas Fine Art. Offices in London, Singapore, Geneva, and Buenos Aires. The ICO launched in October 2017.

What problem is your business attempting to solve?

Maecenas is an online art platform that provides access and liquidity to the fine art investment market by tokenising artworks and selling them as shares, which can in turn be traded on the Maecenas online trading platform.

How developed is your use case (e.g. minimum viable product, proof of concept etc.*)?*

We have released an alpha version of the platform. The beta pilot is soon to be launched where we will initiate our first live auction via a smart contract.

Which blockchain are you using and how are you using it (i.e. what is in the blocks and what is off-chain, public or private)?

Maecenas will run its own private blockchain to maintain artwork provenance records. Transaction records will also be kept on a private blockchain and hashed to the ethereum blockchain at regular intervals.

Business Model and Value System

How important is blockchain technology to your business model and why? Please consider value proposition; market; operations; and finances:

- *Value proposition (i.e. the reason a specific group of customers come to you rather than a competitor)*:
  We have built a robust technical interface for the efficient trading of art shares, backed a strong legal and compliance framework. There is no other marketplace that offers trading in fine art shares. Maecenas is the first art investment platform that opens up access to fine art investment of multi-million-dollar paintings at attainable prices.
- *Market (i.e. your customers, your relationships with those customers, and your channels for reaching those customers, before, during and after a sale)*:
  Our customers include a younger generation of high-net-worth individuals who have become accustomed to and expect the ease of making online transactions. As sophisticated investors, they also appreciate the access to market data that our platform can provide, so they can make informed decisions about how to best manage their investment portfolio. The tokenised fractional approach that we can offer, with the use of the blockchain, gives our customers

the autonomy, allowing them [to] diversify their investment baskets and to react in a timely manner to any movements in the market.

- *Operations (i.e. your human, intellectual, financial and physical resources, your day-to-day activities, and your partnerships)*:
  Operationally, the day-to-day functions required for the expected to democratise fine art and bring art investment to a wider global audience of smaller ticket sizes would not be feasible without the use of technology. Depending on manual processes, the man-hours required alone would be cost prohibitive, which is probably part of the reason why it has not been done before.
- *Finances (i.e. your revenue streams and cost structure)*:
  Maecenas plays the role of marketplace and 'matchmaker' for fine art sellers and buyers. We charge a small fee of 2% to buyers and 6% to sellers for each successful transaction. This is much lower than the current margins charged by galleries and auction houses that can be as high as 25% of the sale price. The historically high commission rates reflect the current monopoly of trust held by these longstanding institutions—trust that can be democratised with the use of the blockchain to increase transparency. We will be accepting both fiat and cryptocurrencies on the platform, which will be converted into our own utility token, ART, which will act as a base currency for clearing and also necessary for the technology and smart contracts to run.

How important is blockchain technology to your value system (i.e. the value chain as it extends beyond your specific company to suppliers, distributors and customers) and why?

[No answer on the record]

Opportunities, Barriers, Risks

What do you consider the main benefits that blockchain technology can offer, both to your business and across your industry more broadly?

Blockchain technology offers multiple improvements in efficiency to an industry that has traditionally depended on solely manual processes. Art sales information has been notoriously opaque or privy to only a handful of selected experts due to the private nature of many sales. This information asymmetry makes it difficult for interested new investors to break into the art market. Blockchain can provide an open and transparent database of provenance for global artworks, it keeps a record of all transactions when art shares and bought and sold, thus maintaining a reliable pricing record for the art industry.

What do you consider the main barriers to adoption, both within your company and beyond, and how might those barriers be overcome? Please consider political, economic, social, technological, legal and/or environmental factors.

This is a completely new model that has never been done before in the art market, and one of the biggest challenges we had was to ensure that from legal and compliance standpoint we had a firm and strong infrastructure for the asset-backed securities. However, we are consistently receiving encouraging feedback and validation from experts in the industry who are just as excited as we are about the new direction and opportunities that Maecenas can provide to revolutionise the art investment market and the industry as a whole.

What do you consider the risks—to your company and beyond—of adopting blockchain technology? Again, please consider political, economic, social, technological, legal and/or environmental factors.

A huge benefit of blockchain technology is security—there is very low risk of manipulation and [it] is robust from a regulatory standpoint due to its transparent nature. The flip side of this is that as custodians of the disclosed information, we are very mindful of our customers' data privacy, which is why we keep all personal information stored on a private blockchain which cannot be accessed by the public. With any new technology, there may also be resistance from incumbents who are likely to adopt a wait-and-see approach. We are confident, however, that the wealth of benefits that the blockchain can bring will be more than sufficient to convince all industry players of its practical application.

Final Questions

What do you see as the likely timeline, both for your company and for the broader adoption of blockchain technology?

Maecenas is currently focusing on launching our auction platform for shares in fine art. We are launching the beta platform in June. Based on the feedback we get from our community of beta testers, we intend to continue to refine the auction platform for the official soft launch, which will be followed shortly after by the launch of the trading platform. Fine art is just the beginning. If the tokenised structure proves to be an effective and popular investment model—and we believe it will be—it can be applied to a range of illiquid asset classes, such as precious gems, vintage cars, fine wines, luxury collectibles etc.

What is the biggest misconception about adopting blockchain technology within the creative industries?

One of the biggest misconceptions about blockchain is that bitcoin and blockchain are one and the same. A blockchain is a technological tool, and each blockchain can be built differently and designed to serve different purposes. Although, bitcoin was the first and perhaps most well-known use of blockchain technology, they are very different things—bitcoin is a cryptocurrency; blockchain technology records peer-to-peer transactions in real time. With this common misconception comes the other false assumption that blockchains are used by criminals who want to remain anonymous. Cryptocurrencies are actually some of the most traceable currencies on the planet, as every transaction is recorded, and cannot be altered or deleted.

What one step could policy-makers take to promote the adoption of blockchain technology in the creative industries in what you would consider a positive manner?

There is currently very little in way of clear guidelines regarding the adoption of blockchain technology, the guidelines that do exist also vary significantly from one jurisdiction to the next. Imposed regulatory restrictions are paradoxical, as the basic premise of the blockchain was designed to be self-regulating and self-governing. So perhaps the best approach for regulators to promote the technology is to remain open-minded to this fast-growing technology and allow it to grow organically.

Company: Publica

Interview respondent: Josef Marc (CEO)

Introduction

Please state the name of your business, its location(s), and the year in which it was launched.

Publica. A Gibraltar corporation with offices in Riga, Latvia. 2017.

What problem is your business attempting to solve?

1. Book authors, their publishers, and book buyers (readers) don't have ecommerce in the cryptocurrency space.
2. Traditional digital book solutions—Digital Rights Management technology and End User License Agreements (DRM/EULA)—don't support buyers' digital ownership or readers' rights.

How developed is your use case (e.g. minimum viable product, proof of concept etc.*)?*

Book ICOs are underway. Ereader-wallet apps are in use by readers. Roadmap is ahead of schedule announced in Publica's ICO. ('ICO' is a common vernacular in the blockchain space, often used colloquially or as jargon. ICO was originally an acronym for Initial Coin Offering. At Publica, Book ICO means an announced and scheduled period when a book's token is first offered for sale by the author or publisher. At the end of a Book ICO, Publica writes that book's smart contract to the blockchain. There are no 'coins' involved in most ICOs, including Publica's Book ICOs. Instead, tokens, typically ethereum ERC20 tokens, are sold. Publica's ICO was held in November 2017 and sold about 18 million PBL tokens to the public. PBL tokens are used as currency in the Publica protocol, so in colloquial terms PBL could be considered a coin.)

Which blockchain are you using and how are you using it (i.e. what is in the blocks and what is off-chain, public or private)?

- Ethereum.
- Publica's currency is called Pebbles, PBL ticker, ERC20. Books are bought with Pebbles.
- Books are access-controlled with Book Tokens in Publica's apps. ERC20.
- Book ICOs are defined in ethereum smart contracts written by Publica at the conclusion of each Book ICO.
- Book metadata are stored in AWS [Amazon Web Services]. Book metadata are presented in Publica apps and on shop.publica.com.
- Publica ereader-wallet app holds buyer's Book Tokens. ERC20. Transferable—this is the digital ownership feature.
  - When Book Tokens are transferred as a gift, viz., no commerce, sender pays ethereum gas.
  - When Book Tokens are resold, viz., ecommerce, this represents a secondary market in digital books. The author's/publisher's smart contract on ethereum may include a portion of resale revenue to the author/publisher.
- Book contents are received from authors/publishers in standard epub format. They're encrypted and stored on AWS. Publica apps consult ethereum smart contract public keys before rendering book contents in the Publica apps. Authors/publishers have the option to

request from Publica an on-chain book storage solution on another blockchain [or peer-to-peer hypermedia protocol] like IPFS.

Business Model and Value System
How important is blockchain technology to your business model and why? Please consider value proposition; market; operations; and finances:

- *Value proposition (i.e. the reason a specific group of customers come to you rather than a competitor)*:
    - Competitors in crowdfunding—because they don't support cryptocurrencies or Book ICOs.
    - Competitors in crypto space—because they don't include an ereader-wallet app that controls book digital ownership.
- *Market (i.e. your customers, your relationships with those customers, and your channels for reaching those customers, before, during and after a sale)*:
    - Customer segment—famous authors—personal relationship with Publica's CEO. Reached through industry word of mouth. Before a sale—we consider their Book ICO to be a sale in this context—we discuss the co-marketing and definition of their Book ICO. After a sale, we discuss co-marketing and their next Book ICO.
    - Customer segment—independent creative entrepreneurs—online relationship with Publica and Publica's Author Advisor Sukhi Jutla (she's also an independent creative author published on Publica). Channels include the Alliance of Independent Authors, appearances at book fairs and author events, YouTube interviews, Telegram authors channel, and author newsletter from Publica. Before a sale, it's FAQ and author information about how to register their Book ICO. After a sale—during their Book ICO—Publica gathers email addresses from opt-in registrants. After their Book ICO, authors/publishers receive those registrants' emails for their own platforms.
    - Customer segment—readers and Book ICO participants—online relationship with Publica's community managers in Europe, Asia, North America. Channels include Telegram, Twitter, Facebook, Discord, YouTube, interviews, mainstream press, crypto press, Publica email newsletters. Before a sale (Book ICO) they're informed about upcoming events and Book ICOs.

- *Operations (i.e. your human, intellectual, financial and physical resources, your day-to-day activities, and your partnerships)*:
  - Publica is a spinoff of Scandiweb.com, a full stack vertical agency. Full-time human resources are 10.
  - Intellectual resources include advisors with relevant qualifications in authorship (authors), academics (digital economy professors), economics (adjunct scholar to Mises Institute), and governance in the crypto space (a public speaker on the topic of crypto space governance).
- *Finances (i.e. your revenue streams and cost structure)*:
  - Publica retains 10% of PBL transactions (book sales).
  - Publica pays costs of Book ICOs and ethereum smart contracts.
  - Publica pays for marketing Book ICOs and maintaining publica.com. Authors and publishers also market their Book ICOs (called co-marketing).
  - Publica develops and maintains the Publica ereader-wallet apps.
  - Publica develops and maintains the AWS back end infrastructure.

How important is blockchain technology to your value system (i.e. the value chain as it extends beyond your specific company to suppliers, distributors and customers) and why?

- Suppliers—authors and publishers—ethereum smart contracts represent a cost reduction, particularly in revenue distribution and accounting.
- Distributors—n/a, Publica is its own distributor. Unless you count personal device makers like Android and iOS; they're indifferent to the Publica project, it's just another app to them.
- Customers—book buyers/readers—ERC20 Book Tokens represent digital ownership of a book. This was first demonstrated in 'the token heard around the world' [a project in which Jules Verne's *Around the World in 80 Days* was passed from wallet to wallet, ereader to ereader, with full its itinerary recorded on a blockchain].

Opportunities, Barriers, Risks
What do you consider the main benefits that blockchain technology can offer, both to your business and across your industry more broadly?

- Our business—Digital ownership. It's a differentiator from all previous DRM/EULA technologies.
- Industry—Introduction of cryptocurrencies and book tokens. Digital ownership applies as well, because of the introduction of secondary markets for digital books. Cryptocurrencies because they represent a new marketplace and outlet for books. Blockchains because they're independent of territories defined by legacy practices developed for shipping paper books.

What do you consider the main barriers to adoption, both within your company and beyond, and how might those barriers be overcome? Please consider political, economic, social, technological, legal and/or environmental factors.

- Political—Government regulators don't normally think about books. They do think about copyrights per the WIPO [World Intellectual Property Organisation] and Berne Convention derivatives. Publica Book Tokens are fully compliant with the WIPO and Berne Convention but it will take time for political bodies to think that through. They're not interfering with Publica in any way at this time.
- Economic—Most mainstream book buyers don't have cryptocurrency yet. Publica is introducing a 'fiat layer' to its apps so they won't have to own cryptocurrency to buy a book. Authors will receive PBL tokens as payment. They seem to be OK with selling PBL for other currencies on their own time.
- Social—Where TV and internet news feed the general public with fears of blockchain fraud, mainstream adoption may associate Book ICOs and Book Tokens with bitcoin and other [crypto]coins, despite no direct connection. Book ICOs by famous authors will soothe those fears.
- Technological—Ethereum is a public peer-to-peer network serving many stakeholders. In the future, it may evolve to be less suitable to Book ICOs and Book Tokens particularly in transaction costs and speed. Publica is prepared to move its protocol to other blockchains if necessary to serve its customers well.
- Legal—India, for example, prohibits authors and publishers from holding cryptocurrencies. This prevents them from being able to use the Publica project, despite their keen interest and

demonstrated expertise. Publica can't do anything about that. Also in legal, Publica can't be a bank or hold authors'/publishers' PBL tokens for them, so we're educating them about the importance of caring for their own digital wallets.

- Environmental—We've been asked about the electricity use of bitcoin and ethereum, although Publica's use of ethereum is negligible compared to coins who rely on it for many (many) more transactions. We know that the blockchain community in general is concerned too, and is working to improve blockchain technology to reduce that energy use.

What do you consider the risks—to your company and beyond—of adopting blockchain technology? Again, please consider political, economic, social, technological, legal and/or environmental factors.

I don't mean to be flip, but we don't consider blockchain technology to be a risk, simply because we don't know any alternative way to implement Book ICOs and digital ownership to book buyers' digital wallets-ereaders.

Final Questions

What do you see as the likely timeline, both for your company and for the broader adoption of blockchain technology?

- Broader adoption for our company—Adoption will be steady and that's all we seek. Books are already globally adopted. Publica Book Tokens will find their natural place in that adoption. Timeline—We'll announce annual results at Frankfurt Book Fair in October.
- Broader adoption for blockchain technology—In our CEO's experience in USA, WWW [World Wide Web] adoption (web pages, not the internet in general) took about four years. We think blockchain technology will take a similar period. Awareness of blockchain technology is going much faster than the WWW's was, but we liken it more to the adoption of using credit cards in WWW ecommerce. Television news told people to never put their credit card numbers into a website, and that held back adoption. Television news tells people that blockchains are rife with criminal activity, similar to credit card fraudsters in the WWW adoption era. So the timeline is likely lying in the public's time to see through TV news *schadenfreude*, and best practices to be deployed, tested, proven, and errors fixed and publicised.

What is the biggest misconception about adopting blockchain technology within the creative industries?

Subjective answer—That copyrights are somehow involved. They're not. Copyrights are defined by 'first tangible form' and its timestamp. Those are created by the first computer that hosts the content, and take legal precedence over any blockchain's timestamp or ledger. Taken in copyright's companion, piracy, creatives often think that piracy limits their revenue. Books are different from songs, TV, and movies. Textual content is freely shared by authors and publishers in their marketing and publicity. Books are a reading experience. Although pirated books exist, they're not an ecommerce market like songs, TV, movies. Copyright violation lawsuits are rare in books, and blockchain technology wouldn't apply anyway (see 'first tangible form'). Nonetheless, creatives are reassured by Publica's Book Tokens, digital ownership restricted to the buyer's digital wallet, secondary markets with revenue-share to the rights holder(s), and the three pairs of cryptographic keys we use in the Publica protocol.

What one step could policy-makers take to promote the adoption of blockchain technology in the creative industries in what you would consider a positive manner?

Clearly distinguish between copyright, piracy, and token ownership. The general public already understands tokens in other forms like airplane boarding passes, concert tickets etc. Build on that.

Company: Verisart

Interview respondent: Robert Norton (CEO & Founder)

Introduction

Please state the name of your business, its location(s), and the year in which it was launched.

Verisart, Los Angeles & London, 2015.

What problem is your business attempting to solve?

Digital certificates of authenticity for physical artworks and collectibles.

How developed is your use case (e.g. minimum viable product, proof of concept etc.)?

Growing partner revenues and already working with leading artists and arts organisations such as Shepard Fairey, DACS [Design and Artists

Copyright Society], Paddle 8, Avant Arte, Art Systems, Fonderia Nolana and many others.

Which blockchain are you using and how are you using it (i.e. what is in the blocks and what is off-chain, public or private)?

Bitcoin blockchain.

Business Model and Value System

How important is blockchain technology to your business model and why? Please consider value proposition; market; operations; and finances:

- *Value proposition (i.e. the reason a specific group of customers come to you rather than a competitor)*:
  We combine the best in classification standards for cultural objects, blockchain certification and image recognition in an easy to use platform designed for artists, dealers and collectors.
- *Market (i.e. your customers, your relationships with those customers, and your channels for reaching those customers, before, during and after a sale)*:
  We provide a Partner Certification Program for companies wishing to use our blockchain certification and verification platform for their art and collectibles. The program allows partners to use our Partner API and to fully customise their certificates.
- *Operations (i.e. your human, intellectual, financial and physical resources, your day-to-day activities, and your partnerships)*:
  As we are a fast-growing business this changes frequently and it would be best to check our website for the latest information.
- *Finances (i.e. your revenue streams and cost structure)*:
  Not for publication.

How important is blockchain technology to your value system (i.e. the value chain as it extends beyond your specific company to suppliers, distributors and customers) and why?

It's essential.

Opportunities, Barriers, Risks

What do you consider the main benefits that blockchain technology can offer, both to your business and across your industry more broadly?

Verisart is a simple way for artists to register their works on the blockchain. When an artist creates a work, a digital certificate containing important information such as the artwork image, title, artist name, signature, year of production and materials is encrypted and recorded forever. It helps artists and collectors secure the value of their works and create trusted title. Unlike traditional paper records, these digital certificates of authenticity cannot be duplicated and this significantly reduces the scope for fraudulent activity and fake copies.

What do you consider the main barriers to adoption, both within your company and beyond, and how might those barriers be overcome? Please consider political, economic, social, technological, legal and/or environmental factors.

Our two biggest challenges are getting the art market to fully adopt distributed ledger technologies and promoting the widespread use of digital certification as part of the transaction of an artwork.

What do you consider the risks—to your company and beyond—of adopting blockchain technology? Again, please consider political, economic, social, technological, legal and/or environmental factors.

Emerging technologies are fraught with potential risks as protocols evolve, new blockchains emerge and the legislative landscape remains uncertain. Getting people to do things for the first time requires a mindset shift and one should not underestimate the challenge of gaining widespread consumer adoption without meaningful and easy to use blockchain applications.

Final Questions

What do you see as the likely timeline, both for your company and for the broader adoption of blockchain technology?

We're experiencing strong traction since the start of 2018 and expect this to continue throughout the next five years as people become more comfortable with the use and application of distributed ledger technologies.

What is the biggest misconception about adopting blockchain technology within the creative industries?

Smart contracts and neither necessarily smart nor contracts in a legal sense. They are better described as self-executing code based on pre-agreed parameters.

What one step could policy-makers take to promote the adoption of blockchain technology in the creative industries in what you would consider a positive manner?

They could recognise blockchain certificates as legal verifiable claims.

Index

M. O'Dair, *Distributed Creativity*,
https://doi.org/10.1007/978-3-030-00190-2

The manufacturer's authorised representative in the EU is Springer Nature Customer Service Centre GmbH, Europaplatz 3, 69115 Heidelberg, Germany. If you have any concerns regarding our products, please contact ProductSafety@springernature.com

Printed and bound by CPI Group (UK) Ltd, Croydon, CR0 4YY
22/09/2026
02221067-0019